Celebrate
Country Woman
Christmas 1998

I t's family and food…fond memories and fun projects…meeting new friends and reflecting on the reason for the season.

Christmas comes once a year. And again *this* year, we've collected the very best parts of it for you.

You see, *Country Woman Christmas 1998* is truly a celebration of Christmas from the heart of the country. Almost all the recipes, photos, stories and craft ideas have come to us directly from the readers of *Country Woman* magazine. Here's a brief look at what awaits you.

Dig in! Busy country cooks become even more active as the holidays approach. But not too busy to share their very best holiday recipes!

From appetizers to desserts, this keepsake book brings you over 100 never-before-published hearty recipes to add to your festive file. Each had to pass a rigorous taste test in the *Country Woman* kitchen—plus an equally important *time* test.

At Christmastime, there's no time to spare for extra trips to town. So—like those in *Country Woman* itself—*every* recipe in this book can be made with ingredients most cooks keep on hand.

***Quick* Crafts, Too.** Similarly, *Country Woman Christmas 1998* contains dozens of original holiday craft projects—with instructions, patterns and charts—that take no more than a few hours to finish…yet will brighten your home and gift-giving long after this season ends.

You'll also enjoy cheerful profiles of country women who find special ways to bring the holidays home, peeks at the way others decorate for the season that'll provide you with exciting new ideas for your own home, true stories of the beauty of Christmas, touching poems from country Christmas-loving folks just like you—and many more delightful features and photos.

More in Store. With a colorful new edition being added to this series every year, you can look forward to many more country-flavored holiday celebrations. But, for now, simply settle back with *Country Woman Christmas 1998*. We hope you enjoy it as much as we've enjoyed bringing it to you!

Senior Editor
Kathy Pohl

Food Editor
Coleen Martin

Associate Food Editor
Sue A. Jurack

Assistant Food Editor
Corinne Willkomm

Test Kitchen Home Economist
Julie Seguin

Test Kitchen Assistants
Judith Scholovich
Suzi Hampton

Craft Editors
Jane Craig
Tricia Coogan

Associate Editors
Kathleen Anderson
Sharon Selz
Faithann Stoner
Kristine Krueger

Editorial Assistant
Sarah Grimm

Art Directors
Vicky Marie Moseley
Tom Hunt
Gail Engeldahl

Art Associate
Nancy Krueger

Photographers
Scott Anderson
Glenn Thiesenhusen

Food Photography Artist
Stephanie Marchese

Photo Studio Manager
Anne Schimmel

Production Assistants
Claudia Wardius
Ellen Lloyd

© 1998 Reiman Publications, L.P.
5400 S. 60th Street
Greendale WI 53129

International Standard Book Number:
0-89821-234-0
International Standard Serial Number:
1093-6750

All rights reserved.
Printed in U.S.A.

INSIDE...

AND MUCH MORE!

PICTURED ON OUR COVER. Clockwise from top left: Popcorn Almond Brittle (p. 37), Wood Santa Necklace (p. 82), Coffee Stirrer Sticks (p. 45), Christmas Card Box (p. 98), Appliqued Poinsettia Place Mat (p. 66), Roly-Poly Santas (p. 30), Chocolate Reindeer (p. 34), Clay North Pole Pals (p. 89).

Photo Contributors: p. 7—Shanie Veenendaal, Debbie Karppinen; p. 56—Tom Martin; p. 105—Carolyn Moser; p. 106—Sandra Siens Wallin, J.R. Wallin; p. 107—Betty and Yvette Ward; p. 108—Marvin Riddle, John Friedman; p. 110—Tom Harper.

Readers' Poetry Corner

Christmas Eve Magic

Long stockings hang waiting, arranged in a row
By three eager youngsters with eyes all aglow.
Neat hand-printed notes, each with special request,
Are pinned to the stockings, to "SANTA" addressed.

Hot cocoa and cookies stacked on a large plate
Say "thank you" to Santa for being so great…
And child-crafted baubles on fir tree displayed
Were hung by the same little hands they were made.

Gifts under the tree, though imperfectly tied,
Were chosen with love and were wrapped up with pride.
The story of Christmas once more has been read
And bedtime prayers whispered, each child tucked in bed.

How blessed is the home in which young ones reside—
There wonder and reverence for Christmas abide!

—*Louise Pugh Corder*
Franklinville, North Carolina

Tasty Decorating Highlights Her Homes for the Holidays

JUST AS with Santa himself, house calls are a big part of the holidays for farm wife Teri Harwood.

"Folks start phoning in orders for my gingerbread houses in early autumn," the happy homemaker and grandmother of four from rural George, Washington grins. "By mid-November, a month-long 'construction season' has begun in my kitchen."

Teri's Christmas carpentry dates back 14 years, to when she first made gingerbread houses as gifts for family and friends. Soon, her all-edible edifices began attracting purchasers. Her holidays have been full of ginger ever since.

"I've baked as many as 50 houses in a season," she says. "A Swiss chalet, Santa's house and a classic candy cottage are among my favorites. I've also made a Noah's ark, barn, carousel, manger and sleigh. No two of them are ever exactly alike.

"I bake and cut all the pieces for several houses first, then assemble them with 'mortar' of white frosting. To complete the scene, I add snow-white icing and colorful candy."

And what a sweet scene it is! "I use peppermint swirl shingles, pretzel fences, red-hot cobblestones and candy cane chimneys," she lists as she trims. "In addition, I add tiny electric lights. They look so festive, reflecting through my lollipop windows.

"I can easily go through 150 pounds of flour, 100 pounds of powdered sugar, 48 pounds of shortening and 15 pounds of gumdrops in a season. Some people display the same house year after year. But for families with children, gingerbread's meant for nibbling."

A busy partner to her husband, Bill, Teri admits her wintry confections take a fair bite from her schedule. "Luckily, for us, gingerbread making is a family affair," she notes.

"My mother and daughters often help with decorating, and Bill and the grandkids are my head taste-testers. Friends and neighbors stop in to lend a hand, too. They say they just follow their noses straight to the kitchen!"

As for what most spice up *her* life, the yummiest rewards come from others, Teri shares: "I love to watch the faces of wide-eyed children when they spot a gingerbread house."

Editor's Note: *If you'd like a copy of her gingerbread house recipe, send a self-addressed stamped envelope to Teri Harwood, 17041 Rd. 4 NW, Quincy WA 98848.*

RAISING THE ROOF with her baking, farm wife Teri Harwood finds family's gingerbread house business is a piece of holiday cake.

WELCOME TO MY COUNTRY KITCHEN

By Ardis Weiss of Sherburn, Minnesota

NORWEGIAN NOEL. Dressed in traditional costume of Norway, Ardis Weiss (above left) serves festive feast honoring family's Scandinavian roots. Above, elf rides herd on straw goat beneath butcher block.

EACH CHRISTMAS, my kitchen takes on a distinctly different flavor…one that comes all the way from Scandinavia!

I enjoy trimming the heart of our century-old farmhouse with merry accents that reflect my Norwegian and Swedish heritage. And my whole family—husband Lyle, our three grown children and seven grandchildren—looks forward to the beautiful result.

Actually, displaying rural "roots" is something I do year-round here in the kitchen and adjacent sun porch. Both are filled with antique farm furniture and implements, among them some treasured tinware from Lyle's mother.

It's a warm, homespun look I like to call "early attic"—and it provides the right background for the bright ethnic embellishments I add during the holidays.

Front and Center

The old-time butcher block in the middle of the kitchen is the first to undergo a Yuletide transformation. A small flocked evergreen and grinning *nisse* (Norwegian elf) dress it up. On the braided rug covering my brick-like linoleum floor below the butcher block stands a straw goat bearing another *nisse*, all surrounded by greenery.

Especially at this time of year, when making treats takes top priority many days, I appreciate the convenience of my kitchen. Everything's at hand—from cooking supplies inside the cupboards covered with custom-made pine doors to my well-used oven and spacious off-white counters, where I prepare such delicacies as *krumkake* (crispy cookies) and *julekake* (a yeast bread filled with candied fruits).

Since food plays such a big part in our festivities, one of my favorite tasks is decking the dining table on the sun porch. I layer it with red plaid fabric, then a jute topper featuring Swedish figures, followed by woven heart mats.

Temporarily retiring our everyday dishes, I set the table with Porsgrund "Heart and Pine" china, a Norwegian brand I found locally. Printed napkins tucked inside heart rings and a Swedish centerpiece fashioned from straw finish the scene.

Figuring in More Fun

Cavorting among the decorated tools, tins and baskets tucked in and around the Hoosier cupboard and old icebox on the porch is a group of gnome-like characters. Those engaging fellows—called *tomtes*—also dance about amid sprigs of pine on the windowsills, providing a cheery frame for the view of our snow-covered farm.

To bring some of that outdoor beauty in, I put up a spruce covered in ornaments, including a string of miniature flags. Many of the items on the tree are gifts from friends and relatives who know of my affinity for the "Old Country".

8

CHRISTMAS KITCHEN. Tree trimmed with straw ornaments, tiny flags (above) brightens area by Hoosier. Gaily topped table (at right) sports Swedish centerpiece. Elsewhere, elves, trolls, gnomes are at home!

Our celebration hits its peak on December 24. Before heading to church, we all gather to exchange gifts and enjoy the smorgasbord arranged on the kitchen counters. Coffee cakes, lingonberry spread, fruit soup, herring, meatballs and more pile high on plates. I even dress myself up for the occasion by donning a traditional costume from Norway called a *bunad*.

It's been delightful sharing my specially seasoned kitchen with you. I hope its Scandinavian trappings and colorful touches help to brighten *your* Christmas, too. Happy holidays!

BEAUTIFUL BRUNCH! Starting clockwise from top: Swiss Omelet Roll-Up (p. 11), Sparkling Oranges (p. 12), Black Forest Waffles (p. 11) and Swedish Cardamom Rolls (p. 11).

Holiday Brunch

SWISS OMELET ROLL-UP
Gertrude Dumas, Athol, Massachusetts
(Pictured on page 10)

My family always enjoys this scrumptious and unique omelet on Christmas morning after we've opened gifts. Its special taste and appearance make the preparation time worthwhile.

1-1/2 cups mayonnaise,* *divided*
   2 tablespoons all-purpose flour
  12 eggs, *separated*
   1 cup milk
1/2 teaspoon salt
1/8 teaspoon pepper
   6 tablespoons chopped green onions, *divided*
   1 tablespoon Dijon mustard
1-1/2 cups chopped fully cooked ham
   1 cup (4 ounces) shredded Swiss cheese
Fresh oregano *or* parsley, optional

In a saucepan, combine 1/2 cup mayonnaise and flour. In a bowl, whisk egg yolks until thickened; add milk. Pour into mayonnaise mixture; cook over low heat, stirring constantly, until thick. Add salt and pepper. Remove from the heat; cool for 15 minutes. In a mixing bowl, beat egg whites until stiff. Fold into the mayonnaise mixture. Line a 15-in. x 10-in. x 1-in. baking pan with waxed paper; coat paper with nonstick cooking spray. Pour egg mixture into pan. Bake at 425° for 20 minutes. Meanwhile, in a saucepan over low heat, combine 2 tablespoons onions, mustard and remaining mayonnaise. Remove 3/4 cup for topping; set aside and keep warm. To the remaining sauce, add ham, cheese and remaining onions; cook over low heat until cheese begins to melt. Remove omelet from oven; turn onto a linen towel. Peel off waxed paper. Spread cheese sauce over warm omelet. Roll up from a short side. Top with reserved mustard sauce. Garnish with oregano or parsley if desired. Serve immediately. **Yield:** 10-12 servings. ***Editor's Note:** Light or fat-free mayonnaise may not be substituted for regular mayonnaise.

SWEDISH CARDAMOM ROLLS
Betty Slavin, Omaha, Nebraska
(Pictured on page 10)

Raisins, walnuts, orange peel and cardamom give these golden, tender sweet rolls real holiday appeal. Guests are often surprised to learn they're homemade!

   2 packages (1/4 ounce *each*) active dry yeast
3/4 cup warm water (110° to 115°)
   1 cup warm milk (110° to 115°)
3/4 cup sugar
1/2 cup shortening
   2 eggs
   2 tablespoons grated orange peel
   1 to 1-1/2 teaspoons ground cardamom
   1 teaspoon salt
   6 to 6-1/2 cups all-purpose flour

1/2 cup raisins
1/2 cup chopped walnuts
Additional raisins
1/4 cup butter *or* margarine, melted

In a mixing bowl, dissolve yeast in water. Add milk, sugar, shortening, eggs, orange peel, cardamom, salt and 3-1/2 cups flour; beat until smooth. Stir in raisins, walnuts and enough remaining flour to form a soft dough. Turn onto a floured surface; knead until smooth and elastic, about 6-8 minutes. Place in a greased bowl; turn once to grease top. Cover and let rise in a warm place until doubled, about 1 hour. Punch dough down; divide into thirds. Roll each portion into a 12-in. x 10-in. rectangle. Divide in half to form two 12-in. x 5-in. rectangles. Cut each into twelve 5-in. x 1-in. strips; roll strips into 6-in. ropes. To shape rolls, place two ropes on a greased baking sheet to form an X. Coil each end toward the center. Press a raisin into the center of each coil. Cover and let rise until almost doubled, about 30 minutes. Bake at 400° for 8-10 minutes or until golden brown. Brush with butter. **Yield:** 3 dozen.

BLACK FOREST WAFFLES
Edith Johnson, Fruita, Colorado
(Pictured on page 10)

With their dark chocolate flavor and cherry and cream topping, these waffles add a fancy touch to brunch with very little effort.

1-3/4 cups cake flour
   6 tablespoons sugar
   1 tablespoon baking powder
1/2 teaspoon salt
   2 eggs, *separated*
   1 cup milk
   2 squares (1 ounce *each*) unsweetened baking chocolate
   3 tablespoons shortening
   1 cup whipping cream, whipped
   3 tablespoons confectioners' sugar
   1 can (21 ounces) cherry pie filling
Fresh mint, optional

In a mixing bowl, combine flour, sugar, baking powder and salt. Combine egg yolks and milk; stir into dry ingredients. In a double boiler or microwave, melt the chocolate and shortening. Add to batter; mix well. In another mixing bowl, beat egg whites until stiff peaks form; fold into the batter. Bake in a preheated waffle iron according to manufacturer's directions until browned. Combine whipped cream and confectioners' sugar. Serve waffles topped with whipped cream and pie filling. Garnish with mint if desired. **Yield:** 5 waffles (about 6-3/4 inches).

● Enhance the flavor of pancake or waffle batter by adding 1/2 teaspoon cinnamon and nutmeg to the dry ingredients and 1/2 teaspoon vanilla extract to the wet ingredients.

SPARKLING ORANGES
Janie Bush, Weskan, Kansas
(Pictured on page 10)

We were living in Texas when I found the recipe for this simple yet elegant salad. I was thrilled—we had a surplus of fresh oranges! Since it's prepared ahead, there's no last-minute fuss.

    8 large oranges, peeled and sectioned
    1/2 cup sugar
    1/2 cup orange marmalade
    1 cup white grape juice
    1/2 cup lemon-lime soda
    3 tablespoons slivered almonds, toasted
    3 tablespoons flaked coconut, toasted

Place orange sections in a large bowl. In a saucepan, combine sugar and marmalade; cook and stir over medium heat until sugar is dissolved. Remove from the heat. Stir in grape juice and soda. Pour over oranges and toss to coat. Cover and refrigerate overnight. Using a slotted spoon, remove oranges to a serving dish. Sprinkle with almonds and coconut. **Yield:** 8 servings.

PECAN BUTTER
Gladys Chancellor, Laurel, Mississippi

I came up with this rich, nutty spread as a way to jazz up toast. But my big family also looks for it on my holiday brunch buffet. It's a festive topper for muffins, biscuits, rolls and even slices of pound cake.

    2 cups finely chopped pecans
    1 cup butter or margarine, softened
    1/2 cup confectioners' sugar

In a bowl, combine all ingredients; stir until creamy. Store in the refrigerator. **Yield:** 2 cups.

GINGERBREAD PANCAKES
Debbie Baxter, Gresham, Oregon

Christmas breakfast is extra festive when these fragrant spiced pancakes are on the menu. We've even made them in the shape of gingerbread men.

    1 cup all-purpose flour
    1 tablespoon sugar
    1 teaspoon baking powder
    1 teaspoon ground ginger
    1/2 teaspoon ground cinnamon
    1/2 teaspoon baking soda
    1/2 teaspoon salt
Pinch ground cloves
    1 cup buttermilk
    1 egg
    2 tablespoons molasses
    1 tablespoon vegetable oil
Maple syrup and whipped cream, optional

In a mixing bowl, combine the first eight ingredients. Combine buttermilk, egg, molasses and oil; add to dry ingre-
dients and mix well. Pour batter by 1/4 cupfuls onto a lightly greased hot griddle; turn when bubbles form on top of pancakes. Cook until second side is golden brown. Serve with syrup and whipped cream if desired. **Yield:** 8-10 pancakes.

MERRY CHRISTMAS MUFFINS
Ada Kirkland, Saskatoon, Saskatchewan

These moist, fruity muffins are packed with hearty ingredients and spread with a creamy orange-flavored frosting. Served with coffee, they're a favorite with Christmas guests.

    2 cups all-purpose flour
1-1/4 cups sugar
    2 teaspoons baking soda
1-1/2 teaspoons ground cinnamon
    1/2 teaspoon salt
    3 eggs
    1 cup vegetable oil
    2 teaspoons vanilla extract
    2 cups grated carrots
    1 medium tart apple, peeled and chopped
    1/2 cup shredded coconut
    1/2 cup chopped dried mixed fruit
    1/2 cup raisins
FROSTING:
    3 tablespoons butter or margarine, softened
    1 package (3 ounces) cream cheese, softened
2-1/2 cups confectioners' sugar
    1/2 teaspoon orange juice
    1/2 teaspoon vanilla extract
Chopped candied cherries

In a large bowl, combine the first five ingredients. In a small bowl, beat eggs, oil and vanilla; stir into dry ingredients just until moistened. Fold in carrots, apple, coconut, fruit and raisins. Fill paper-lined muffin cups three-fourths full. Bake at 350° for 30 minutes or until muffins test done. Cool for 10 minutes; remove from pan to a wire rack to cool completely. For frosting, combine butter, cream cheese, sugar, juice and vanilla in a mixing bowl; beat until smooth and creamy. Spread over muffins. Sprinkle with cherries. **Yield:** 16 muffins.

OLD-FASHIONED DOUGHNUT HOLES
Mrs. Ron Swift, Mapleton, Minnesota

Light and yummy, these doughnut holes go fast! Their old-time goodness comes from mashed potatoes and buttermilk.

1-1/2 cups hot mashed potatoes (mashed with milk and butter)
    2 cups sugar
    1 cup buttermilk
    3 eggs
    1/3 cup butter or margarine, melted
    1 teaspoon vanilla extract
5-1/2 cups all-purpose flour
    4 teaspoons baking powder
1-1/2 teaspoons baking soda

1 teaspoon salt
1 teaspoon ground cinnamon *or* nutmeg
Oil for deep-fat frying
Additional sugar

In a large bowl, combine the potatoes, sugar, buttermilk, eggs, butter and vanilla. Combine flour, baking powder, baking soda, salt and cinnamon; stir into potato mixture. Refrigerate for 1 hour. In a skillet or electric fry pan, heat 1 in. of oil to 375°. Drop batter by rounded teaspoonfuls into oil; fry until browned. Turn with a slotted spoon. Drain on paper towels. Roll in sugar while warm. **Yield:** 13 dozen.

PUMPKIN COFFEE CAKE
Hazel Fritchie, Palestine, Illinois

I created this recipe when I had surplus pumpkin and was looking for something different to serve for the holidays.

TOPPING:
1/4 cup packed brown sugar
1/4 cup sugar
1/2 teaspoon ground cinnamon
2 tablespoons cold butter *or* margarine
1/2 cup chopped pecans
CAKE:
1/2 cup butter *or* margarine, softened
1 cup sugar
2 eggs
1 cup (8 ounces) sour cream
1/2 cup canned *or* cooked pumpkin
1 teaspoon vanilla extract
2 cups all-purpose flour
1 teaspoon baking soda
1 teaspoon baking powder
1/2 teaspoon pumpkin pie spice
1/4 teaspoon salt

In a small bowl, combine sugars and cinnamon. Cut in the butter until mixture resembles coarse crumbs. Stir in pecans; set aside. In a mixing bowl, cream butter and sugar. Add eggs, one at a time, beating well after each addition. Combine the sour cream, pumpkin and vanilla; mix well. Combine dry ingredients; add to creamed mixture alternately with sour cream mixture. Beat on low just until blended. Spread the batter into two greased and floured 8-in. round cake pans. Sprinkle with topping. Bake at 325° for 40-50 minutes or until a toothpick inserted near the center comes out clean. **Yield:** 16-20 servings.

TWO-CHEESE SPINACH QUICHE
Patricia Nazaruk, Michigan Center, Michigan

This beautiful pie really stars on my holiday brunch buffet. The cheese, ham and spinach flavors blend perfectly. It's easy to prepare besides.

1 unbaked pie pastry (9 inches)
1/2 cup finely shredded Swiss cheese
1/2 cup chopped fresh spinach
1/2 cup sliced fresh mushrooms
1 can (5 ounces) fully cooked ham, flaked

3 eggs
1 cup half-and-half cream
2 teaspoons all-purpose flour
1/2 teaspoon salt
1/4 cup shredded cheddar cheese

Line the unpricked pastry shell with a double thickness of heavy-duty foil. Bake at 450° for 5 minutes. Remove foil. Bake 5 minutes longer. Remove from the oven; reduce heat to 350°. Combine Swiss cheese, spinach, mushrooms and ham; sprinkle over crust. In a bowl, beat eggs, cream, flour and salt until smooth; pour over spinach mixture. Sprinkle with cheddar cheese. Bake for 40-45 minutes or until a knife inserted near the center comes out clean. **Yield:** 6-8 servings.

SAUSAGE ROLLS
Rita Sherman, Coleville, California

Handy packaged crescent rolls and prepared sausages make this finger food quick and easy for breakfast or brunch.

1 tube (8 ounces) refrigerated crescent rolls
8 brown-and-serve sausage links, cooked
1/8 teaspoon garlic powder
1/8 teaspoon rubbed sage
1 egg
1 tablespoon water
Dried parsley flakes
Paprika

Unroll crescent roll dough and separate into four rectangles; seal perforations. Place two sausage links end to end along the long side of each rectangle. Sprinkle with garlic powder and sage. Roll up jelly-roll style and seal the seam with water. Place seam side down on an ungreased baking sheet. In a bowl, beat egg and water; brush over rolls. Sprinkle with parsley and paprika. Cut into 2-in. pieces. Bake at 375° for 11-13 minutes or until golden brown and heated through. **Yield:** about 1 dozen.

STUFFED FRENCH TOAST
Heidi Wilcox, Lapeer, Michigan

Kids like to help stuff the sausage and cheese into the bread, so this is a good holiday treat. I serve it year-round for breakfast when we have guests or on special family occasions.

1 package (8 ounces) brown-and-serve sausage patties
6 slices Italian bread (1-1/2 inches thick)
3 slices Muenster *or* brick cheese, halved
4 eggs
1 cup milk
1 tablespoon sugar
Maple syrup

In a skillet, cook sausage until browned; drain. Cut a pocket in the crust of each slice of bread. Stuff a sausage patty and slice of cheese into each pocket. In a shallow bowl, beat eggs, milk and sugar. Soak bread for 2 minutes. Fry on a greased griddle over medium heat until golden brown on both sides. Serve with syrup. **Yield:** 6 servings.

Christmas Breads

OLD-FASHIONED MINI PLUM LOAVES
Laura Andrew, Newaygo, Michigan

Moist and golden, these loaves are a "plum" part of the holiday baskets our family makes up for country friends and neighbors. I discovered the recipe in a historical cookbook—it truly is full of old-fashioned goodness.

>   2 cups all-purpose flour
> 1-1/2 cups sugar
>   1 teaspoon baking soda
>   1 teaspoon ground cinnamon
>   1/2 teaspoon salt
>   1/4 teaspoon ground nutmeg
>   3 eggs
>   2 jars (4 ounces *each*) plum baby food
>   1/2 cup vegetable oil
>   1 cup chopped pecans *or* walnuts
> TOPPING:
>   1/2 cup sugar
>   1/4 cup buttermilk
>   1/4 cup butter *or* margarine
>   1/2 teaspoon vanilla extract
>   1/2 teaspoon baking soda

In a large bowl, combine the first six ingredients. Stir in eggs, baby food, oil and nuts just until moistened. Spoon into four greased 5-in. x 3-in. x 2-in. loaf pans. Bake at 325° for 40-45 minutes or until a toothpick inserted near the center comes out clean. In a saucepan, combine topping ingredients; bring to a boil. Boil and stir for 3 minutes. Poke holes with a fork in top of loaves; spoon hot topping over hot loaves. Cool in pans for 10 minutes or until topping is absorbed. Remove to wire racks to cool. **Yield:** 4 mini loaves.

CINNAMON WALNUT CRESCENTS
Jessie Alpert, Louisville, Kentucky

Mainstays in my holiday baking are these classic Christmas crescents. Nutty and spicy-sweet, they're ideal for a breakfast buffet. I also tuck them into plates of homemade goodies.

>   3 egg yolks
>   1 cup (8 ounces) sour cream
>   1 package (1/4 ounce) active dry yeast
>   3 cups all-purpose flour
>   1/2 teaspoon salt
>   1 cup cold butter *or* margarine
>   1 cup finely chopped walnuts
>   1 cup sugar
>   2 teaspoons ground cinnamon
> Confectioners' sugar icing, optional

In a small bowl, beat yolks; stir in sour cream and yeast. Let stand for 10 minutes. In a large bowl, combine flour and salt; cut in butter until mixture resembles coarse crumbs. Add sour cream mixture and stir well. Shape into a ball; cover with plastic wrap and refrigerate 8 hours or overnight. Combine walnuts, sugar and cinnamon; sprinkle a fourth of the

mixture on a flat surface. Divide dough into four portions; set three aside. On walnut-sprinkled surface, roll one portion into an 8-in. circle; turn dough over and press walnut mixture into both sides. Cut into 16 wedges. Roll up each wedge into a crescent shape, starting with the wide end. Place point down 1 in. apart on greased baking sheets. Repeat three more times with remaining walnut mixture and dough. Bake at 350° for 20-25 minutes or until golden brown. Cool on wire racks. Drizzle with icing if desired. **Yield:** about 5 dozen. **Editor's Note:** This dough does not require rising time.

FESTIVE BRIOCHES
Diane Halferty, Tucson, Arizona
(Pictured below)

I love creating recipes, and these light and luscious rolls are among my holiday originals. Sometimes I'll substitute chocolate or butterscotch chips, raisins and cherries.

>   1 package (1/4 ounce) active dry yeast
>   1/4 cup warm water (110° to 115°)
>   1/2 cup butter *or* margarine, softened
>   1/3 cup plus 1 tablespoon sugar, *divided*
>   1 teaspoon salt
>   4 cups all-purpose flour
>   1/2 cup milk
>   4 eggs
>   1/2 cup dried cranberries
>   1/2 cup chopped candied pineapple
>   1/4 cup dried currants

In a small bowl, dissolve yeast in water; let stand for 5 minutes. In a mixing bowl, cream butter, 1/3 cup sugar and

salt. Add 1 cup flour and milk. Separate one egg; refrigerate egg white. Add yolk and remaining eggs to the creamed mixture. Stir in the yeast mixture, fruit and remaining flour. Spoon into a greased bowl. Cover and let rise in a warm place until doubled, about 1-1/2 hours. Cover and refrigerate overnight. Punch dough down; turn onto a floured surface. Divide into four portions. Divide three of the portions into eight pieces each. Shape into balls and place in well-greased muffin cups. Divide remaining dough into 24 small balls. Make a depression in the top of each large ball; place a small ball in each depression. Cover and let rise in a warm place until doubled, about 45 minutes. Beat reserved egg white and remaining sugar; brush over rolls. Bake at 375° for 15-20 minutes or until golden brown. Remove from pans; cool on a wire rack. **Yield: 2 dozen.**

NUTTY CREAM CHEESE BISCUITS
Claudia Beene, Bossier, Louisiana

These nutty biscuits are worth every bit of the time they take to prepare. Their rich taste and creamy texture make requests for seconds routine.

    2 tubes (10 ounces *each*) refrigerated biscuits
    2 packages (3 ounces *each*) cream cheese
1/2 cup sugar
    1 teaspoon ground cinnamon
1/4 teaspoon *each* ground cloves, nutmeg and
      allspice
    6 tablespoons butter *or* margarine, melted, *divided*
    1 cup chopped pecans

Roll each biscuit into a 3-1/2-in. to 4-in. circle. Cut cream cheese into 20 equal cubes; place one cube in the center of each biscuit. Combine sugar, cinnamon, cloves, nutmeg and allspice; sprinkle 1/2 teaspoonful over each biscuit. Set remaining sugar mixture aside. Moisten edges of dough with water; fold over cheese and press edges with a fork to seal. Pour 2 tablespoons butter each into two 9-in. cake pans; sprinkle 1 tablespoon of reserved sugar mixture into each. Dip one side of each biscuit in remaining butter. Arrange in pans, forming a pinwheel pattern, with butter side up. Sprinkle pecans and remaining sugar mixture on top. Bake at 375° for 20-25 minutes or until golden brown. Serve warm. **Yield: about 1-1/2 dozen.**

ALMOND APRICOT BREAD
Debbie Tarzwell, Maryland Heights, Missouri

This versatile quick bread is best savored slowly. It's a breakfast loaf, dessert and food gift—all in one. I also like to use the buttery crumb topping on pies, coffee cakes and muffins.

1-1/2 cups water
    1 cup chopped dried apricots
    5 cups all-purpose flour
    2 cups sugar
    7 teaspoons baking powder
1-1/2 teaspoons salt
1-1/2 teaspoons grated orange peel
    1/2 teaspoon baking soda
    2 eggs

    1 cup milk
1/3 cup vegetable oil
3/4 cup orange juice
    1 cup chopped almonds
CRUMB TOPPING:
    2/3 cup all-purpose flour
    1/2 cup confectioners' sugar
Pinch salt
    1/4 cup cold butter *or* margarine
    1/2 teaspoon vanilla extract

In a small saucepan, bring water and apricots to a boil. Cover; remove from the heat and let stand for 10 minutes. Drain, reserving 3/4 cup apricot liquid; set apricots aside. In a large bowl, combine flour, sugar, baking powder, salt, orange peel and baking soda. In another bowl, combine eggs, milk, oil, orange juice and reserved apricot liquid. Stir into dry ingredients just until moistened. Fold in the almonds and apricots. Pour into two greased 9-in. x 5-in. x 3-in. loaf pans. In a small bowl, combine flour, confectioners' sugar and salt; cut in butter until mixture resembles coarse crumbs. Stir in vanilla. Sprinkle over loaves. Bake at 350° for 1 hour or until a toothpick inserted near the center comes out clean. Cool on a wire rack. **Yield: 2 loaves.**

ZUCCHINI ANISE BREAD
Dorothy Olivares, El Paso, Texas

Bushels of late-summer zucchini always put me in the Christmas spirit—thanks to this garden-fresh holiday bread I make. The anise lends a unique licorice-like flavor and fragrance to every piece…and the zucchini gives it such a moist texture.

    3 cups all-purpose flour
    2 cups sugar
    2 tablespoons wheat germ, toasted
    1 teaspoon baking soda
    1 teaspoon salt
    1 teaspoon ground cinnamon
1/2 to 1 teaspoon aniseed
    1/4 teaspoon baking powder
    1 cup vegetable oil
1/4 cup buttermilk
    2 eggs, lightly beaten
    2 teaspoons vanilla extract
1-2/3 cups shredded peeled zucchini
    1 cup chopped walnuts
    1 cup raisins
1/3 cup shredded carrot

In a large bowl, combine the first eight ingredients. In another bowl, combine oil, buttermilk, eggs and vanilla. Add to dry ingredients; mix well. Stir in zucchini, walnuts, raisins and carrot. Spoon into two greased 8-in. x 4-in. x 2-in. loaf pans. Bake at 350° for 1 hour or until a toothpick inserted near the center comes out clean. Cool for 10 minutes; remove from pans to wire racks to cool completely. **Yield: 2 loaves.**

  ● When making yeast bread, after the first rising, press two fingers 1/2 inch into the dough. If the dents remain, the dough is doubled in size and ready to punch down.

FESTIVE BREADS. Clockwise from top right: Onion French Bread (p. 18), Cherry Lattice Coffee Cake (p. 19), Tomato Mini Muffins (p. 19), Orange Cinnamon Bread (p. 18) and Fruited Swedish Tea Ring (p. 18).

FRUITED SWEDISH TEA RING
Betty Murray, Hamiota, Manitoba
(Pictured on page 16)

I entered this festive tea ring in our agricultural fair, and it won top honors. Every year, I make around 15 of the tasty "wreaths" to give as fresh-from-the-kitchen gifts.

FILLING:
1 cup chopped candied fruit
1/2 cup raisins
2/3 cup packed brown sugar
1/4 cup butter *or* **margarine, melted**
1 teaspoon grated orange peel
1/2 teaspoon ground cardamom
DOUGH:
1 package (1/4 ounce) active dry yeast
1-1/4 cups warm water (110° to 115°), *divided*
1/3 cup sugar, *divided*
2 eggs
1/4 cup shortening
1-1/2 teaspoons salt
4-1/4 to 4-3/4 cups all-purpose flour
ICING:
1 cup confectioners' sugar
1 tablespoon lemon juice
1 tablespoon milk
Candied cherries, optional

Combine filling ingredients in a bowl; cover and refrigerate. For dough, combine yeast, 1/4 cup water and 1 teaspoon sugar; let stand for 5 minutes. In a mixing bowl, combine remaining water and sugar; stir until dissolved. Add yeast mixture, eggs, shortening, salt and 3 cups flour; mix until smooth. Add enough remaining flour to form a soft dough. Turn onto a floured surface; knead until smooth and elastic, about 6-8 minutes. Place in a greased bowl, turning once to grease top. Cover and let rise in a warm place until doubled, about 1-1/2 hours. Punch dough down; divide in half. Roll each portion into a 16-in. x 9-in. rectangle. Sprinkle filling over dough to within 1 in. of edge. Tightly roll up, jelly-roll style, starting with a long side; seal ends. Place on greased baking sheets; pinch ends together to form a ring. With a scissors, cut from outside edge two-thirds of the way toward center of ring at 1-in. intervals. Separate strips slightly; twist to allow filling to show. Cover and let rise until doubled, about 1 hour. Bake at 350° for 20-25 minutes or until golden brown. Cool on wire racks for 20 minutes. In a small mixing bowl, beat confectioners' sugar, lemon juice and milk until smooth. Drizzle over tea rings while warm. Decorate with cherries if desired. **Yield:** 2 tea rings.

ORANGE CINNAMON BREAD
Cindy Anderson, Delhi, New York
(Pictured on page 16)

Instead of wrapping up presents to give at Christmas, I customarily knead them. This citrusy cinnamon bread is a hit with anyone who has a sweet tooth. You can also make a loaf that's terrific for toasting by eliminating the glaze.

2 packages (1/4 ounce *each***) active dry yeast**
1/4 cup warm water (110° to 115°)
1 cup milk

3/4 cup orange juice
1 cup sugar, *divided*
1 tablespoon grated orange peel
1-1/2 teaspoons salt
1 egg
6-1/2 to 7 cups all-purpose flour
Additional water
2 teaspoons ground cinnamon
GLAZE:
1 cup confectioners' sugar
2 tablespoons orange juice

In a mixing bowl, dissolve yeast in water; let stand for 5 minutes. In a saucepan, heat milk and orange juice to 110°; add to yeast mixture. Stir in 1/2 cup sugar, orange peel, salt, egg and 3 cups flour; beat until smooth. Add enough remaining flour to form a soft dough. Turn onto a floured surface; knead until smooth and elastic, about 6-8 minutes. Place in a greased bowl, turning once to grease top. Cover and let rise in a warm place until doubled, about 1 hour. Punch dough down; divide in half. Roll each portion into a 15-in. x 7-in. rectangle. Brush with water. Combine cinnamon and remaining sugar; sprinkle over dough to within 1 in. of edge. Tightly roll up, jelly-roll style, starting with a short side; seal ends. Place seam side down in two greased 9-in. x 5-in. x 3-in. loaf pans. Cover and let rise in a warm place until doubled, about 1 hour. Bake at 350° for 35-40 minutes or until golden brown. Remove from pans to cool on a wire rack. Combine glaze ingredients; drizzle over bread. **Yield:** 2 loaves.

ONION FRENCH BREAD
Sandi Pichon, Slidell, Louisiana
(Pictured on page 17)

Holiday meals are even more memorable when I complement them with this chewy onion bread. Day-old slices taste great with soup and sandwich fillings, too.

5 to 5-1/2 cups all-purpose flour
1 envelope onion soup mix
2 packages (1/4 ounce *each***) active dry yeast**
3 tablespoons sugar
2 teaspoons salt
2 cups warm water (120° to 130°)
2 tablespoons shortening
1 egg white
1 tablespoon water

In a mixing bowl, combine 2 cups flour, soup mix, yeast, sugar and salt; add warm water and shortening. Beat on medium speed for 3 minutes. Add enough remaining flour to form a soft dough. Turn onto a floured surface; knead until smooth and elastic, about 3 minutes. Place in a greased bowl, turning once to grease top. Cover and let rise in a warm place until doubled, about 1 hour. Punch dough down; knead 4-5 times. Divide in half. Roll each portion into a 14-in. x 6-in. rectangle. Roll up, jelly-roll style, starting with a long side; pinch edges and ends to seal. Place seam side down on a greased baking sheet. Beat egg white and water; brush over loaves. Cover with plastic wrap that has been sprayed with nonstick cooking spray; let rise until doubled, about 30-40 minutes. With a sharp knife, make four shallow diagonal cuts across the top. Bake at 375° for 30-35 minutes or until golden brown. Cool on a wire rack. **Yield:** 2 loaves.

TOMATO MINI MUFFINS
Retha Cobb, Dothan, Alabama
(Pictured on pages 16 and 17)

It's delightful at Christmas to savor the big bite of summer baked into these scrumptious muffins. Munching one warm from the oven reminds me of plump sun-kissed tomatoes and herbs handpicked from the patch.

1-3/4 cups all-purpose flour
1/3 cup grated Parmesan cheese
2 tablespoons sugar
2 teaspoons baking powder
1/4 to 1/2 teaspoon dried rosemary, crushed
1/4 teaspoon baking soda
1/8 teaspoon garlic powder
1/8 teaspoon pepper
1 egg
1/2 cup milk
1/2 cup tomato sauce
1/3 cup vegetable oil
Additional Parmesan cheese, optional

In a large bowl, combine the first eight ingredients. In another bowl, beat egg. Add milk, tomato sauce and oil; mix well. Stir into the dry ingredients just until moistened. Fill greased or paper-lined miniature muffin cups two-thirds full. Sprinkle with Parmesan cheese if desired. Bake at 375° for 10-12 minutes or until muffins test done. **Yield:** 3 dozen.

CHERRY LATTICE COFFEE CAKE
Mrs. Otto Stank, Pound, Wisconsin
(Pictured on page 17)

This cheery coffee cake is an all-time favorite with my seven grandchildren. The latticed top showcases the cherries so beautifully that it's almost too pretty to eat.

1 package (1/4 ounce) active dry yeast
1/4 cup warm water (110° to 115°)
1 cup (8 ounces) sour cream
1 egg
3 tablespoons sugar
2 tablespoons butter *or* margarine, softened
1 teaspoon salt
3 cups all-purpose flour
FILLING:
2-1/2 cups fresh *or* frozen pitted tart cherries, thawed, rinsed and drained
1/2 to 3/4 cup sugar
1/2 cup chopped almonds, toasted
2 tablespoons all-purpose flour
Dash salt

In a mixing bowl, dissolve yeast in water; let stand for 5 minutes. Add sour cream, egg, sugar, butter, salt and 2 cups flour; beat until smooth. Add enough remaining flour to form a soft dough. Turn onto a floured surface; knead until smooth and elastic, about 6-8 minutes. Place in a greased bowl, turning once to grease top. Cover and let rise in a warm place until doubled, about 1 hour. Punch dough down. Reserve 1 cup dough. Divide remaining dough in half. Roll each portion into a 9-in. circle; place in greased 9-in. round baking pans. Combine filling ingredients; spread over dough to within 1/2 in. of edge. Roll out reserved dough to 1/4-in. thickness; cut into 1/2-in. strips. Make a lattice top over filling. Cover and let rise until doubled, about 45 minutes. Bake at 375° for 15 minutes. Cover top with foil; bake 20 minutes longer or until browned. **Yield:** 2 coffee cakes.

CHOCOLATE NUT BREAD
Jennifer Reisinger, Sheboygan, Wisconsin

You can't go wrong with my grandmother's chocolaty bread recipe. It tastes as yummy as it looks…it's my most-requested special-occasion bread…and it never lasts long at bake sales.

1 cup butter *or* margarine, softened
2 cups sugar
5 eggs
2 squares (1 ounce *each*) unsweetened chocolate, melted
1 teaspoon vanilla extract
2-1/2 cups cake flour
1 teaspoon baking soda
1/4 teaspoon salt
1 cup buttermilk
1 cup chopped walnuts, optional

In a mixing bowl, cream butter and sugar. Add eggs, chocolate and vanilla; mix well. Combine the flour, baking soda and salt; add to creamed mixture alternately with buttermilk, beating well after each addition. Stir in nuts if desired. Pour into four greased 5-in. x 3-in. x 2-in. loaf pans. Bake at 350° for 35 minutes or until a toothpick inserted near the center comes out clean. Cool for 10 minutes; remove from pans to wire racks to cool completely. **Yield:** 4 mini loaves.

GINGER MUFFINS
Erlene Cornelius, Spring City, Tennessee

For fun, I give my friends this recipe along with a do-it-yourself muffin kit. It includes oven-ready batter in a decorative jar and a few finished muffins to nibble as a sample.

1/2 cup shortening
1 cup sugar
2 eggs
1 cup molasses
3 cups all-purpose flour
2 teaspoons ground cinnamon
1 teaspoon ground ginger
1 teaspoon baking powder
1 teaspoon baking soda
1 teaspoon salt
1 cup sour milk*

In a mixing bowl, cream shortening and sugar. Add eggs and molasses; mix well. Combine dry ingredients; add to creamed mixture alternately with sour milk, mixing just until blended. Fill greased muffin cups half full. Bake at 350° for 16-20 minutes or until muffins test done. Cool for 10 minutes; remove from pans to wire racks to cool completely. **Yield:** 2-1/2 dozen. ***Editor's Note:** To sour milk, place 1 tablespoon white vinegar in measuring cup; add enough milk to measure 1 cup.

APPEALING APPETIZERS! Top to bottom: Hot Apple Punch (p. 21), Pinecone-Shaped Spread (p. 21), Artichoke Dip (p. 21) and Bacon Rounds (p. 21).

Appetizers

PINECONE-SHAPED SPREAD
Lisa Pointer, Leadore, Idaho
(Pictured on page 20)

Spreading Christmas cheer is deliciously simple with this holiday novelty. Originally my mother's recipe, it always gets raves.

    1 package (8 ounces) cream cheese, softened
    1/2 cup mayonnaise
    5 bacon strips, cooked and crumbled
    1 tablespoon finely chopped green onion
    1/2 teaspoon dill weed
    1/8 teaspoon pepper
  1-1/4 cups whole unblanched almonds, toasted
  Fresh rosemary sprigs, optional
  Assorted crackers *or* raw vegetables

In a bowl, combine the cream cheese, mayonnaise, bacon, onion, dill and pepper; chill. Form into two pinecone shapes on a serving platter. Beginning at the narrow end of each shape, arrange almonds in overlapping rows. Garnish with rosemary if desired. Serve with crackers or vegetables. **Yield:** 1-1/2 cups.

HOT APPLE PUNCH
Dawn Supina, Edmonton, Alberta
(Pictured on page 20)

With its soothing cinnamon seasoning, this fresh and flavorful apple punch is a must for Christmastime.

    2 cinnamon sticks (about 3 inches *each*), broken
   10 whole cloves
    6 whole allspice *or* 2 whole nutmeg
    2 quarts apple juice
  Additional cinnamon sticks, optional

Place the cinnamon sticks, cloves and allspice on a double thickness of cheesecloth; bring up the corners and tie with string to form a bag. Place in a large saucepan with apple juice (or place loose spices in pan and strain before serving). Bring to a boil. Reduce heat; cover and simmer for 30 minutes. Remove spice bag. Serve punch hot in mugs. Garnish with cinnamon sticks if desired. **Yield:** 2 quarts.

ARTICHOKE DIP
Mrs. William Garner, Austin, Texas
(Pictured on page 20)

Crackers make great dippers for this creamy appetizer (chips and breadsticks work well, too). It's become the traditional introduction to our family's Christmas Eve dinner.

    1 can (14 ounces) artichoke hearts, drained and
      chopped
    1 cup mayonnaise
  1/3 to 1/2 cup grated Parmesan cheese

    1 garlic clove, minced
  Dash hot pepper sauce
  Paprika, optional
  Assorted crackers

In a bowl, combine the artichokes, mayonnaise, Parmesan cheese, garlic and hot pepper sauce. Transfer to a greased 1-qt. baking dish. Sprinkle with paprika if desired. Bake, uncovered, at 300° for 30 minutes. Serve warm with crackers. **Yield:** 2 cups.

BACON ROUNDS
Edie Despain, Logan, Utah
(Pictured on page 20)

On my family's list of favorite nibbles, this appetizer is tops. I've served the satisfying canapes at showers and brunches.

    1 cup mayonnaise *or* salad dressing
    1 tablespoon grated Parmesan cheese
    2 teaspoons Worcestershire sauce
  1/4 teaspoon paprika
  1/8 teaspoon celery seed
  1/8 teaspoon garlic powder
  1/8 teaspoon pepper
    2 cups (8 ounces) shredded cheddar cheese
    8 bacon strips, cooked and crumbled
  1/3 cup chopped salted peanuts
    4 green onions, thinly sliced
   24 small French bread slices *or* 12 slices white bread
  Additional sliced green onions, optional

In a bowl, combine the first seven ingredients; mix well. Stir in cheese, bacon, peanuts and onions; mix well. Spread over bread. Sprinkle with additional onions if desired. Place on ungreased baking sheets. Bake at 400° for 8-10 minutes or until lightly browned. If using white bread, cut into quarters. **Yield:** 4 dozen. **Editor's Note:** Rounds may be frozen before baking. Bake at 400° for 10-12 minutes or until lightly browned (they do not need to be thawed first).

HOT MUSTARD POPCORN
Diane Hixon, Niceville, Florida

When friends pop in at Yuletide, I like to dish up yummy munchies like this one. Mixed with zippy seasoning, it's best enjoyed with a thirst-quenching beverage.

    1 teaspoon ground mustard
  1/2 teaspoon dried thyme
  1/2 teaspoon salt
  1/4 teaspoon pepper
  Dash cayenne pepper
    3 quarts freshly popped popcorn

Combine the first five ingredients. Place popcorn in a large bowl; add seasonings and toss. **Yield:** 3 quarts.

BREAD POT FONDUE
Terry Christensen, Roy, Utah

Bring this fun fondue to a buffet or potluck and you'll be the toast of the gathering. Folks always ask for the recipe.

    2 cups (8 ounces) shredded cheddar cheese
1-1/2 cups (12 ounces) sour cream
    2 packages (3 ounces *each*) cream cheese, softened
1/4 pound chopped fully cooked ham
1/2 cup finely chopped green onions
    1 can (4 ounces) chopped green chilies
    1 teaspoon Worcestershire sauce
    1 round loaf (1 pound) Italian bread
Raw vegetables, crackers *or* tortilla chips

In a mixing bowl, combine the first three ingredients. Stir in ham, onions, chilies and Worcestershire sauce; set aside. Cut top fourth off loaf of bread; carefully hollow out top and bottom, leaving a 1/2-in. shell. Cube removed bread; set aside. Spoon ham mixture into the bottom shell, mounding slightly. Replace top; wrap tightly with a double layer of heavy-duty foil. Bake at 350° for 1 to 1-1/2 hours. Stir before serving. Serve with reserved bread cubes, vegetables, crackers or tortilla chips. **Yield:** 4 cups.

DILLY SHRIMP
Diana Holmes, Hubertus, Wisconsin

A friend shared the recipe for this delicious hors d'oeuvre. The zesty sauce complements the shrimp nicely and guarantees they'll be gobbled up.

1-1/2 cups mayonnaise
1/2 cup sour cream
1/3 cup lemon juice
1/4 cup sugar
    1 large red onion, thinly sliced
    2 tablespoons dill weed
1/4 teaspoon salt
   32 medium cooked shrimp (about 2 pounds),
      peeled and deveined

In a bowl, combine mayonnaise, sour cream, lemon juice and sugar. Stir in onion, dill, salt and shrimp. Cover and refrigerate for 8 hours or overnight. Serve with toothpicks. **Yield:** 10 servings.

HAM 'N' CHEESE QUICHES
Virginia Abraham, Vicksburg, Mississippi

When I need a festive finger food, this quiche recipe's the one I reach for. With cheese in both the crust and the filling, eating one naturally leads to another.

1/2 cup cold butter *or* margarine
    1 jar (5 ounces) process sharp cheese spread
    1 cup all-purpose flour
    2 tablespoons water
FILLING:
    1 egg
1/2 cup milk

1/4 teaspoon salt
1/2 cup finely chopped ham
1/2 cup shredded Monterey Jack cheese

In a bowl, cut butter and cheese spread into flour until well blended. Add water and toss with a fork until a ball forms. Refrigerate for 1 hour. Press tablespoonfuls onto the bottom and up the sides of greased miniature muffin cups. In a bowl, beat egg, milk and salt. Stir in ham and cheese. Spoon a rounded teaspoonful into each shell. Bake at 350° for 30 minutes or until golden brown. Let stand 5 minutes before serving. **Yield:** 2 dozen.

SAUSAGE BACON TIDBITS
Doris Heath, Bryson City, North Carolina

These taste-tempting tidbits come gift-wrapped. The savory sausage stuffing rolled up in bacon makes an irresistible combination that everyone loves.

1-1/2 cups herb-seasoned stuffing mix
1/4 cup butter *or* margarine
1/4 cup water
1/4 pound bulk pork sausage
    1 egg, beaten
    1 pound sliced bacon

Place stuffing mix in a large bowl. In a saucepan, heat butter and water until butter is melted. Pour over stuffing. Add sausage and egg; mix well. Refrigerate for at least 1 hour. Shape into 1-in. balls. Cut bacon strips in half; wrap a strip around each stuffing ball and secure with a toothpick. Place in an ungreased 15-in. x 10-in. x 1-in. baking pan. Bake, uncovered, at 375° for 20 minutes. Turn; bake 15 minutes longer or until bacon is crisp. Drain on paper towels; serve warm. **Yield:** about 2-1/2 dozen.

CHEESE OLIVE APPETIZERS
Marian Platt, Sequim, Washington

Here's a quick way to dress up a hot roll mix. The tender crust smothered in a saucy cheese topping will make company think that you've fussed.

    1 package (16 ounces) hot roll mix
3/4 cup warm water (110° to 115°)
    1 egg
1/4 cup butter *or* margarine, melted
    1 cup (4 ounces) shredded cheddar cheese
    1 tablespoon poppy seeds
TOPPING:
    2 cups (8 ounces) shredded cheddar cheese
    1 cup sliced stuffed olives
1/3 cup butter *or* margarine, melted
    1 egg, beaten
    1 tablespoon dried minced onion
    1 teaspoon Worcestershire sauce

In a large bowl, dissolve yeast from hot roll mix in warm water. Add egg, butter, cheese and poppy seeds. Add flour from mix; blend well. Press into a greased 15-in. x 10-in. x 1-in. baking pan. Cover and let rise in a warm place until doubled, about 45 minutes. Combine topping ingredients; spread over dough. Bake at 400° for 20-25 minutes or until golden brown. Cut into squares; serve warm. **Yield:** about 4 dozen.

HOLIDAY APPETIZER PUFFS
Kathy Fielder, Dallas, Texas

Good things come in little packages with these melt-in-your-mouth puffs. Besides crabmeat, I've used whipped cream or pudding as the filling to create bite-size desserts.

    1 cup water
    1/2 cup butter *or* margarine
    1 cup all-purpose flour
    1/2 teaspoon salt
    4 eggs
FILLING:
    1 package (8 ounces) cream cheese, softened
    1/4 cup mayonnaise
    1 can (6 ounces) crabmeat, drained and cartilage removed
    1/2 cup shredded Swiss cheese
    1 tablespoon snipped fresh *or* dried chives
    1 teaspoon garlic salt
    1 teaspoon Worcestershire sauce
    1/4 teaspoon pepper

In a heavy saucepan over medium heat, bring water and butter to a boil. Add flour and salt all at once; stir until a smooth ball forms. Remove from the heat; let stand for 5 minutes. Add eggs, one at a time, beating well after each addition. Beat until smooth. Drop by rounded teaspoonfuls 2 in. apart onto greased baking sheets. Bake at 400° for 25-30 minutes or until lightly browned. Immediately cut a slit in puffs to allow steam to escape. Cool on wire racks. When puffs are cool, split and remove soft dough from inside. In a mixing bowl, beat cream cheese and mayonnaise until smooth. Stir in remaining filling ingredients. Spoon into puffs; replace tops. **Yield:** 4 dozen.

FESTIVE TURKEY MEATBALLS
Audrey Thibodeau, Mesa, Arizona

Turkey gives a different twist to these slightly sweet and spicy meatballs. For the holidays, I serve them on a tray lined with parsley and garnished with red pepper or pimientos.

    1 egg, beaten
    1/2 cup dry bread crumbs
    1/4 cup finely chopped onion
    1/2 teaspoon curry powder
    1/4 teaspoon ground ginger
    1/4 teaspoon ground cinnamon
    1/8 teaspoon salt
    1/4 teaspoon pepper
    1 pound ground turkey
SAUCE:
    1 cup honey
    1/4 cup Dijon mustard
    1/2 teaspoon curry powder
    1/2 teaspoon ground ginger

In a bowl, combine the first eight ingredients. Add turkey; mix well. Form into 1-in. balls. Place in a greased 13-in. x 9-in. x 2-in. baking dish. Bake, uncovered, at 350° for 20-25 minutes or until juices run clear. Meanwhile, combine sauce ingredients in a small saucepan; cook and stir until heated through. Brush meatballs with 1/4 cup sauce; return to the oven for 10 minutes. Serve remaining sauce with meatballs for dipping. **Yield:** about 2-1/2 dozen.

EGGNOG DIP
Sharon MacDonnell, Lantzville, British Columbia

I put together a cookbook of my grandma's Christmas recipes that includes this classic eggnog appetizer. Serve it as a dip with fresh fruit or drizzle it over cake for dessert.

    1-1/2 cups eggnog*
    2 tablespoons cornstarch
    1/2 cup sour cream
    1/2 cup whipping cream
    1 tablespoon sugar
    1/2 teaspoon rum extract, optional
Assorted fruit and pound cake cubes

In a saucepan, combine the eggnog and cornstarch until smooth. Bring to a boil; boil and stir for 2 minutes. Remove from the heat; stir in sour cream. Cool completely. In a mixing bowl, beat whipping cream and sugar until stiff peaks form. Fold into eggnog mixture with extract if desired. Cover and refrigerate overnight. Serve with fruit and cake cubes. **Yield:** about 2-1/2 cups. ***Editor's Note:** This recipe was tested with commercially prepared eggnog.

CURRIED CHICKEN TRIANGLES
Anne Marie Cardilino, Kettering, Ohio

Plain refrigerated crescent rolls shape up festively into these time-saving treats. Serve the savory triangles warm, then stand back and watch them vanish.

    2 tubes (8 ounces *each*) refrigerated crescent rolls
    1 can (5 ounces) chunk white chicken, undrained
    1 can (8 ounces) sliced water chestnuts, drained and chopped
    1 cup (4 ounces) shredded Swiss cheese
    1/2 cup chopped green onions
    1/3 cup mayonnaise
    1 teaspoon lemon juice
    1/2 teaspoon curry powder
    1/2 teaspoon garlic salt
Paprika, optional

Separate crescent dough; cut each piece into four triangles. Place on greased baking sheets. In a bowl, break up chicken. Add the water chestnuts, cheese, onions, mayonnaise, lemon juice, curry powder and garlic salt; mix well. Drop by rounded teaspoonfuls onto triangles. Sprinkle with paprika if desired. Bake at 350° for 12-15 minutes or until edges are lightly browned. Serve warm. **Yield:** about 5-1/2 dozen.

> ● Hard cheeses, like Parmesan, are easiest to grate or shred when warm. Semisoft cheeses (cheddar, Swiss and Monterey Jack), on the other hand, are easier to handle when cold.

BUTTERCUP SQUASH BREAD
Mary Merchant, Barre, Vermont

We like this chewy, hearty bread as a substitute for white bread with holiday meals and at breakfast. My five children are grown but still live within "eating distance", so I often bake it in large quantities.

    1 package (1/4 ounce) active dry yeast
1/2 cup warm water (110° to 115°)
    2 tablespoons molasses
    1 teaspoon salt
1/2 to 1 teaspoon caraway seeds
    1 cup mashed cooked buttercup squash
    3 cups all-purpose flour

In a large mixing bowl, dissolve yeast in water. Add molasses, salt, caraway, squash and 2 cups flour; mix well. Add enough remaining flour to form a soft dough. Turn onto a floured surface; knead until smooth and elastic, about 6-8 minutes. Place in a greased bowl, turning once to grease top. Cover and let rise in a warm place until doubled, about 1 hour. Punch dough down; turn onto a floured surface and shape into a loaf. Place in a greased 9-in. x 5-in. x 3-in. loaf pan. Cover and let rise until doubled, about 45 minutes. Bake at 400° for 25-30 minutes or until golden brown. Remove from pan to cool on a wire rack. **Yield:** 1 loaf.

ELEGANT BREAD PUDDING
Sharon Runyan, Fort Wayne, Indiana

At holiday potlucks, our whole family looks forward to my sister-in-law bringing this best-of-the-season dessert. The scrumptious caramel sauce is a unique touch.

  10 cups cubed croissants *or* French bread
1/2 cup raisins
    8 eggs
    2 cups half-and-half cream
    1 cup packed brown sugar
    1 teaspoon ground cinnamon
    1 teaspoon ground nutmeg
    1 teaspoon grated orange peel
CARAMEL SAUCE:
    1 cup packed brown sugar
1/2 cup butter *or* margarine
1/2 cup whipping cream
    1 teaspoon vanilla extract
Whipped cream, optional

Place bread cubes evenly in a greased 13-in. x 9-in. x 2-in. baking dish; sprinkle with raisins. In a large bowl, beat eggs, cream, sugar, cinnamon, nutmeg and orange peel; pour over bread. Bake, uncovered, at 350° for 30 minutes. Cover with foil and bake 15 minutes longer or until a knife inserted near the center comes out clean. In a saucepan, combine the first four sauce ingredients; cook and stir over low heat until smooth. Serve bread pudding in bowls with caramel sauce and whipped cream if desired. **Yield:** 12-14 servings.

ONION-STUFFED ACORN SQUASH
Barb Zamowski, Rockford, Illinois
(Pictured below)

Acorn squash are such a treat this time of year, especially when dressed up for the holidays with a special stuffing. I found this recipe in an old cookbook that was handed down to me.

    3 small acorn squash, halved and seeded
    1 egg, beaten
1/4 teaspoon salt
1/8 teaspoon pepper
    1 teaspoon chicken bouillon granules
    2 tablespoons boiling water
1/4 cup chopped onion
    2 tablespoons butter *or* margarine
    1 cup crushed sage stuffing mix

Invert squash in a greased 15-in. x 10-in. x 1-in. baking pan. Fill pan with hot water to a depth of 1/4 in. Bake, uncovered, at 400° for 30 minutes or until tender. When cool enough to handle, scoop out pulp, leaving a 1/4-in. shell (pulp will measure about 3 cups). Place shells cut side up in a greased 15-in. x 10-in. x 1-in. baking pan; set aside. In a bowl, combine pulp, egg, salt and pepper. Dissolve bouillon in water; add to squash mixture. In a small saucepan, saute onion in butter until tender; stir in stuffing mix. Set aside 1/4 cup for topping; add remaining stuffing mixture to squash mixture. Spoon into shells. Sprinkle with reserved stuffing mixture. Bake, uncovered, at 400° for 20 minutes or until heated through. **Yield:** 6 servings. **Editor's Note:** The squash mixture may be baked in a greased 1-qt. baking dish instead of in the shells.

STUFFED BEEF TENDERLOIN
Marianne Blackman, Fairfield, Connecticut

As spectacular as it is to the eye—with ham, cheese and spinach peeking out of every slice—there's very little fuss to making this main dish. The meat turns out extremely tender, too.

1 beef tenderloin (3 pounds)
Celery salt, garlic powder and pepper to taste
1/4 pound sliced provolone cheese
6 cups fresh spinach
1/2 pound thinly sliced fully cooked ham

Cut a lengthwise slit down the center of the tenderloin to within 3/4 in. of bottom; open tenderloin so it lies flat. Flatten to 1/2-in. thickness. Sprinkle with celery salt, garlic powder and pepper. Layer with cheese, spinach and ham; press down gently. Roll up, starting with a long side; secure with string. Sprinkle with additional celery salt, garlic powder and pepper. Place in a shallow baking pan. Bake, uncovered, at 400° until meat reaches desired doneness, about 35-40 minutes for medium (160°) and 45 minutes for well-done (170°). Let stand 10 minutes before slicing. **Yield: 10-12 servings.**

CHRISTMAS BROCCOLI SALAD
Luann Kessi, Eddyville, Oregon

What could be more Christmasy than a red and green dish? Plus, once people taste this crisp lightly dressed salad, I never have to worry about leftovers.

4-1/2 cups broccoli florets
3 cups chopped sweet red pepper
10 bacon strips, cooked and crumbled
1/3 cup sliced green onions
1/4 cup chopped pecans
3/4 cup mayonnaise
1 tablespoon cider *or* red wine vinegar
Dash pepper

In a large bowl, combine the first five ingredients. In a small bowl, combine the mayonnaise, vinegar and pepper until smooth. Pour over broccoli mixture; toss to coat. Cover and refrigerate until serving. **Yield: 16 servings.**

CRANBERRY DELIGHT
Billie Wilson, Murray, Kentucky

This holiday salad stars cranberries in a tart ruby topping that sits on a snow-white cream cheese layer.

1 cup graham cracker crumbs (about 16 crackers)
1/4 cup butter *or* margarine, melted
2 cups fresh *or* frozen cranberries
1 cup sugar
1/2 cup water
1/3 cup chopped pecans
3 tablespoons orange marmalade
1 package (8 ounces) cream cheese, softened
1/3 cup confectioners' sugar
1 tablespoon milk

1 teaspoon vanilla extract
1 cup whipping cream, whipped

Combine crumbs and butter; press into an ungreased 8-in. square baking dish. Chill. In a saucepan, combine cranberries, sugar and water; bring to a boil. Reduce heat and simmer for 20 minutes. Remove from the heat. Stir in pecans and marmalade; refrigerate until completely cool. Meanwhile, combine cream cheese, confectioners' sugar, milk and vanilla in a mixing bowl; beat until smooth. Fold in whipped cream. Spread over crust. Top with cranberry mixture. Refrigerate for at least 2 hours. **Yield: 8 servings.**

SAVORY ONIONS AND SPINACH
Sue Smith, Norwalk, Connecticut

This delicious mixture of onions and spinach—draped in a rich Parmesan cream sauce—looks as festive as it tastes.

2 pounds frozen pearl onions
1 garlic clove, minced
3 tablespoons butter *or* margarine, *divided*
1 package (10 ounces) fresh spinach*
3/4 cup grated Parmesan cheese, *divided*
1/4 cup whipping cream
Salt and pepper to taste
3 tablespoons dry bread crumbs

Cook onions according to package directions; drain well and set aside. In a saucepan, saute garlic in 2 tablespoons butter for 1-2 minutes. Add spinach; cook and stir until spinach is wilted and liquid evaporates, about 3 minutes. Stir in 1/2 cup of Parmesan cheese and the cream. Stir in onions, salt and pepper. Place in a greased shallow 2-qt. baking dish. Combine bread crumbs and remaining cheese; sprinkle over onion mixture. Dot with remaining butter. Bake, uncovered, at 400° for 20 minutes or until golden brown. Serve with a slotted spoon. **Yield: 8 servings. *Editor's Note:** A 10-ounce package of frozen spinach, thawed and squeezed dry, may be substituted for the fresh spinach.

RED AND GREEN APPLE SALAD
Fayellen McFarlane, Kitimat, British Columbia

Even though this colorful salad is perfect at Christmastime, it's so good I fix it throughout the year for buffets.

3 medium unpeeled green apples, coarsely chopped
3 medium unpeeled red apples, coarsely chopped
2 tablespoons lemon juice
1 cup (8 ounces) sour cream
1/4 cup mayonnaise
1 cup chopped dates
1 cup chopped walnuts
20 red maraschino cherries, halved
20 green maraschino cherries, halved

In a large bowl, toss apples with lemon juice. Cover and refrigerate. Just before serving, combine sour cream and mayonnaise. Pour over apples and toss to coat. Stir in dates, nuts and cherries. **Yield: 10 servings.**

DELIGHTFUL DINING! Clockwise from top right: Holiday Gift Cake (p. 29), Duck with Orange Hazelnut Stuffing (p. 28), Twice-Baked Potatoes Supreme (p. 28), Pork Tenderloin with Mushrooms (p. 28), Carrot Ring (p. 28) and Spectacular Citrus Salad (p. 28).

CARROT RING
Elaine Strassburger, Madison, Wisconsin
(Pictured on page 26)

Carrots become everyone's favorite when they're baked in this slightly sweet, lighter-than-air ring. Our holiday meal wouldn't be complete without it.

    2 pounds carrots, peeled, cooked and mashed
3/4 cup half-and-half cream
    3 eggs, beaten
1-1/2 teaspoons minced fresh parsley
    1 teaspoon finely chopped onion
1/2 teaspoon salt
1/4 teaspoon pepper
    1 package (10 ounces) frozen peas, cooked

Combine the first seven ingredients. Pour into a well-greased 6-cup ring mold. Bake, uncovered, at 350° for 35-40 minutes or until a knife inserted near the center comes out clean. Let stand for 10 minutes; unmold onto a serving plate. Fill the center with peas. **Yield:** 8-10 servings.

SPECTACULAR CITRUS SALAD
Debbie Crutcher, Tulsa, Oklahoma
(Pictured on pages 26 and 27)

A delightfully different salad is what I was looking for when I came across the original version of this recipe. I altered it a bit to fit my taste. Each time I serve this salad, it gets raves for being so colorful and refreshing.

1/2 cup vegetable oil
1/4 cup orange juice
    2 tablespoons honey
    2 tablespoons lime juice
    2 teaspoons poppy seeds
    1 teaspoon grated orange peel
1/2 teaspoon grated lime peel
  12 cups torn red and green leaf lettuce
    3 medium oranges, peeled and sectioned
3/4 cup thinly sliced red onion
2/3 cup pecan halves, toasted

In a jar with tight-fitting lid, combine the first seven ingredients; shake well. In a large salad bowl, combine lettuce, oranges, onion and pecans. Add dressing and toss to coat; serve immediately. **Yield:** 10-12 servings.

PORK TENDERLOIN WITH MUSHROOMS
Dorothe Aigner, Roswell, New Mexico
(Pictured on page 26)

Over the years, I've found the trick to serving this tender pork with its mild onion- and mushroom-flavored gravy is to fix enough—people tend to come back for seconds!

    2 pork tenderloins (about 1 pound *each*)
    3 tablespoons butter *or* margarine
    1 teaspoon salt

1/4 teaspoon pepper
    1 medium onion, thinly sliced
1-1/2 cups sliced fresh mushrooms
1/2 cup thinly sliced celery
    2 tablespoons all-purpose flour
1/2 cup chicken broth
Hot wild rice *or* noodles, optional

In a skillet, brown pork in butter. Transfer meat to an ungreased shallow 1-1/2-qt. baking dish. Sprinkle with salt and pepper; set aside. In the pan drippings, saute the onion, mushrooms and celery until tender. Combine flour and broth until smooth; add to skillet. Bring to a boil; cook and stir for 2 minutes. Pour over meat. Cover and bake at 325° for 1 hour or until a meat thermometer reads 160°-170°. Let stand 5 minutes before slicing. Serve with rice or noodles if desired. **Yield:** 8 servings.

TWICE-BAKED POTATOES SUPREME
Ruth Andrewson, Leavenworth, Washington
(Pictured on pages 26 and 27)

On Christmas Day, we invite all our nearby relatives to dinner. One way I make the meal memorable is with this side dish that combines mashed and baked potatoes.

    8 large baking potatoes
1/4 cup butter *or* margarine, softened
1/2 teaspoon garlic powder
1/2 teaspoon salt
1/2 teaspoon dried oregano
1/4 teaspoon cayenne pepper
1/8 teaspoon celery salt
1/3 to 1/2 cup milk
Grated Parmesan cheese
Paprika, optional

Pierce the potatoes with a fork. Bake at 400° for 60-70 minutes or until tender. Cut potatoes in half lengthwise; scoop out pulp, leaving a thin shell. Set shells aside. In a large bowl, mash pulp; add butter, garlic powder, salt, oregano, cayenne, celery salt and enough milk to make a smooth filling. Stuff or pipe into shells; place in two greased 13-in. x 9-in. x 2-in. baking pans. Sprinkle with Parmesan cheese and paprika if desired. Bake, uncovered, at 350° for 20-25 minutes or until heated through. **Yield:** 16 servings.

DUCK WITH ORANGE HAZELNUT STUFFING
Donna Smith, Victor, New York
(Pictured on page 27)

For over 50 years, this elegant entree has graced my family's holiday table. The zesty stuffing with its nice nutty crunch complements the slices of moist duck, while the hint of orange in the gravy sets it apart.

    2 domestic ducklings (4 to 5 pounds *each*)
    1 teaspoon salt
STUFFING:
    4 cups coarse soft bread crumbs

2 cups chopped peeled tart apple
2 cups chopped toasted hazelnuts
1 cup chopped celery
1/2 cup chopped onion
1/2 cup orange juice
2 eggs, beaten
1/4 cup butter *or* margarine, melted
2 to 3 tablespoons lemon juice
2 teaspoons grated orange peel
1-1/2 teaspoons grated lemon peel
1 teaspoon seasoned salt
1/2 teaspoon pepper
1/2 teaspoon dried thyme
1/4 teaspoon ground nutmeg
Additional butter *or* margarine, melted
GRAVY:
3 tablespoons all-purpose flour
1/4 teaspoon salt
1/8 teaspoon pepper
2 cups chicken broth
1/3 cup orange marmalade

Sprinkle the inside of ducks with salt; prick skin several times and set aside. Combine the first 15 stuffing ingredients; spoon into ducks. Place with breast side up on a rack in a large shallow roasting pan. Brush with butter. Bake, uncovered, at 350° for 2 to 2-1/2 hours or until a meat thermometer reads 180° for duck and 165° for stuffing. Remove all stuffing and keep warm. For gravy, combine 3 tablespoons pan drippings, flour, salt and pepper in a saucepan; stir until smooth. Heat until bubbly, stirring constantly. Gradually add broth. Bring to a boil; cook for 1-2 minutes, stirring constantly. Add marmalade; stir until smooth. Serve with ducks and stuffing. **Yield:** 8 servings.

HOLIDAY GIFT CAKE
Roberta Edwards, Middleboro, Massachusetts
(Pictured on page 27)

More than 25 years ago, to remind my two young children of the real meaning of the season, I decided our Christmas dinner should include a birthday cake. This rich lovely dessert has served that purpose ever since.

1 package (8 ounces) cream cheese, softened
1 cup butter *or* margarine, softened
1-1/2 cups sugar
1-1/2 teaspoons vanilla extract
4 eggs
2-1/4 cups cake flour
1-1/2 teaspoons baking powder
1 jar (8 ounces) maraschino cherries, drained
1/2 cup chopped pecans
GLAZE:
1-1/2 cups confectioners' sugar
2 tablespoons milk
Birthday candles, optional

In a mixing bowl, beat cream cheese, butter, sugar and vanilla until smooth. Add eggs, one at a time, beating well after each addition. Combine flour and baking powder; gradually add 2 cups to batter. Set aside five to six cherries for garnish. Chop the remaining cherries; add to remaining flour mixture with pecans. Fold into batter. Pour into a

greased and floured 10-in. fluted tube pan. Bake at 325° for 1 hour and 20 minutes or until a toothpick inserted near the center comes out clean. Cool for 5 minutes; remove from pan to a wire rack to cool completely. For glaze, combine sugar and milk in a small bowl; stir until smooth. Drizzle over cake. Decorate with reserved cherries and candles if desired. **Yield:** 12 servings. **Editor's Note:** Green maraschino cherries may also be used for garnish.

SWEET POTATO CARROT CRISP
Diane Molberg, Emerald Park, Saskatchewan

Sweet potatoes take a different twist in this whipped side dish that pairs them with carrots. It's subtly sweet and has just a hint of garlic, while the nut and crumb topping adds a fun crunch to any holiday meal.

4 medium sweet potatoes, peeled and cubed
2 pounds carrots, cut into 1/2-inch chunks
3/4 cup orange juice
2 tablespoons honey
2 tablespoons butter *or* margarine
2 garlic cloves, minced
1 teaspoon salt
1 teaspoon ground cinnamon
TOPPING:
3/4 cup soft bread crumbs
1/4 cup chopped pecans
2 to 3 tablespoons butter *or* margarine, melted
2 teaspoons minced fresh parsley

In a large saucepan, cook sweet potatoes and carrots until tender; drain. Cool slightly; place in a blender or food processor. Add orange juice, honey, butter, garlic, salt and cinnamon; cover and process until smooth. Pour into a greased 2-1/2-qt. baking dish. Combine topping ingredients; sprinkle over sweet potato mixture. Cover and bake at 350° for 30 minutes. Uncover; bake 15-20 minutes longer or until heated through. **Yield:** 12-16 servings.

FESTIVE CORN
Joy Beck, Cincinnati, Ohio

For a deluxe side dish that's easy yet has big impact, I whip up this recipe. It features corn and peppers in a comforting cream cheese sauce.

1/4 cup chopped green pepper
1/4 cup chopped sweet red pepper
2 green onions, thinly sliced
2 tablespoons butter *or* margarine
1 package (8 ounces) cream cheese, cubed
2/3 cup milk
3/4 teaspoon salt
1/8 teaspoon pepper
1/2 teaspoon dill weed
1 package (16 ounces) frozen corn, thawed

In a saucepan over medium heat, saute peppers and onions in butter until tender. Add cream cheese, milk, salt, pepper and dill. Cook and stir over low heat until cheese is melted. Add corn; heat through. **Yield:** 6-8 servings.

Holiday Cookies

RAINBOW BUTTER COOKIES
Lanette Tate, Sandy, Utah

Our family can't get through the holidays without these fun, colorful cookies. They come out of my oven by the dozens!

1/2 cup plus 2 tablespoons butter (no substitutes), softened
1/2 cup packed brown sugar
1/4 cup sugar
1 egg
1 teaspoon vanilla extract
2 cups all-purpose flour
1/2 teaspoon baking powder
1/2 teaspoon salt
1/8 teaspoon baking soda
Green, red and yellow food coloring
Milk

In a mixing bowl, cream butter and sugars. Add egg and vanilla; mix well. Combine dry ingredients; gradually add to creamed mixture. Divide dough into three portions; tint each a different color. Roll each portion of dough on waxed paper into a 9-in. x 5-in. rectangle. Freeze for 10 minutes. Cut each rectangle in half lengthwise. Lightly brush top of one rectangle with milk. Top with another colored dough. Remove waxed paper; brush top with milk. Repeat with remaining dough, alternating colors, to make six layers. Press together lightly; cut in half lengthwise. Wrap each with plastic wrap. Chill several hours or overnight. Unwrap dough; cut into 1/8-in. slices. Place 2 in. apart on ungreased baking sheets. Bake at 350° for 8-10 minutes. Cool for 1-2 minutes; remove from pans to wire racks. **Yield:** about 4 dozen.

ANISE SUGAR COOKIES
Paula Marchesi, Rocky Point, New York

As much as I love giving away my baking, a few goodies—like these cookies—are "keepers". The light anise flavor and melt-in-your-mouth texture make them a perfect after-dinner treat.

1 cup butter (no substitutes), softened
1-1/2 cups sugar
2 eggs
1/4 to 1/2 teaspoon anise extract
3 cups all-purpose flour
1 to 1-1/2 teaspoons aniseed
1 teaspoon baking powder
1 teaspoon baking soda
1 teaspoon salt
Frosting and colored sugar, optional

In a mixing bowl, cream butter and sugar. Add eggs and extract; mix well. Combine flour, aniseed, baking powder, baking soda and salt; gradually add to creamed mixture and mix well. Shape into 1-in. balls; place on greased baking sheets. Flatten with a glass dipped in sugar. Bake at 375° for 6-7 minutes. Cool on wire racks. If desired, frost cookies and sprinkle with colored sugar. **Yield:** 9 dozen.

ROLY-POLY SANTAS
Mrs. Andrew Seyer, Oak Ridge, Missouri
(Pictured below)

I tuck one of these fanciful Santas into every gift cookie tray I make. They're a guaranteed hit with kids—young and old. And I like that they're not too difficult to assemble.

1 cup butter (no substitutes), softened
1/2 cup sugar
1 tablespoon milk
1 teaspoon vanilla extract
2-1/4 cups all-purpose flour
Red paste food coloring
Miniature chocolate chips
FROSTING:
1/2 cup shortening
1/2 teaspoon vanilla extract
2-1/3 cups confectioners' sugar, *divided*
2 tablespoons milk, *divided*

In a mixing bowl, cream butter and sugar. Add milk and vanilla; mix well. Add flour and mix well. Remove 1 cup dough; add red food coloring. Shape white dough into 12 balls, 3/4 in. each, and 48 balls, 1/4 in. each. Shape red dough into 12 balls, 1 in. each, and 60 balls, 1/2 in. each. Place the 1-in. red balls on two ungreased baking sheets for the body of 12 Santas; flatten to 1/2-in. thickness. Attach 3/4-in. white balls for heads; flatten to 1/2-in. thickness. Attach four 1/2-in. red balls to each Santa for arms and legs. Attach 1/4-in. white balls to ends of arms and legs for hands and feet. Shape remaining 1/2-in. red balls into hats (see the photo). Add chocolate chip eyes and buttons. Bake at 325° for 12-15 minutes or until set. Cool for 10 minutes; carefully remove from pans to wire racks (cookies will be

fragile). For frosting, combine shortening and vanilla in a small mixing bowl; mix well. Gradually add 1-1/3 cups confectioners' sugar; add 1 tablespoon milk. Gradually add remaining sugar and milk. Fill a pastry bag with frosting. With a round decorator's tip, add a band of icing on hat, cuffs at hands and feet, and down the front and at bottom of jacket. Use a small star tip to pipe beard and pom-pom on hat. **Yield:** 1 dozen. **Editor's Note:** Remaining dough may be shaped into balls and baked.

FRUITCAKE COOKIES
Bonnie Milner, De Ridder, Louisiana

For folks who like their fruitcake in small doses, this is the mouth-watering answer. I always have plenty packed away in the freezer to replenish my Yuletide supply.

     1 cup butter (no substitutes), softened
1-1/2 cups sugar
     2 eggs
2-1/2 cups all-purpose flour
     1 teaspoon baking soda
     1 teaspoon ground cinnamon
  1/2 teaspoon salt
     2 cups chopped pecans
     1 package (8 ounces) chopped dates
     8 ounces candied cherries, halved
     8 ounces candied pineapple, diced

In a mixing bowl, cream butter and sugar. Add eggs; mix well. Combine flour, baking soda, cinnamon and salt; add to creamed mixture and mix well. Fold in pecans, dates and fruit. Drop by rounded teaspoonfuls onto greased baking sheets. Bake at 325° for 13-15 minutes or until lightly browned. Cool on wire racks. **Yield:** 8 dozen.

CHERRY-FILLED COOKIES
Mrs. Delbert Benton, Guthrie Center, Iowa

The luscious cherry filling peeking out of these rounds is just a hint of how scrumptious they are. Using a doughnut cutter to shape each cookie top really speeds up the process.

  1/2 cup shortening
     1 cup packed brown sugar
  1/2 cup sugar
     2 eggs
  1/4 cup buttermilk
     1 teaspoon vanilla extract
3-1/2 cups all-purpose flour
  1/2 teaspoon salt
  1/2 teaspoon baking soda
     1 can (21 ounces) cherry pie filling

In a mixing bowl, cream shortening and sugars. Add eggs, buttermilk and vanilla; mix well. Combine flour, salt and baking soda; gradually add to creamed mixture and mix well. Cover and chill for 1 hour or until firm. Divide dough in half. On a floured surface, roll each portion to 1/8-in. thickness. Cut with a 2-3/4-in. round cutter. Place half of the circles 2 in. apart on greased baking sheets; top each with a heaping teaspoon of pie filling. Cut holes in the center of re-

maining circles with a 1-in. round cutter; place over filled circles. Seal edges. Bake at 375° for 10 minutes or until golden brown. Cool on wire racks. **Yield:** about 3 dozen.

STUFFED DATE DROPS
Clarice Schweitzer, Sun City, Arizona

In my recipe collection, these chewy drop cookies with date-nut centers are filed under "E" for "extra-special".

     12 pecans *or* walnut halves
     24 pitted whole dates
      2 tablespoons butter (no substitutes), softened
   1/3 cup packed brown sugar
      1 egg yolk
   3/4 cup all-purpose flour
   1/4 teaspoon baking powder
   1/4 teaspoon baking soda
   1/3 cup sour cream
BROWN BUTTER FROSTING:
      2 tablespoons butter (no substitutes)
   3/4 cup confectioners' sugar
   1/2 teaspoon vanilla extract
1-1/2 to 2 teaspoons milk

Cut pecan or walnut halves lengthwise; stuff into dates and set aside. In a mixing bowl, cream butter and brown sugar. Beat in egg yolk. Combine flour, baking powder and baking soda; add to creamed mixture alternately with sour cream. Stir in stuffed dates. Drop by tablespoonfuls, with one date per cookie, onto greased baking sheets. Bake at 375° for 7-9 minutes or until golden brown. Cool on wire racks. In a saucepan, cook butter over medium heat until golden brown, about 5 minutes. Gradually stir in sugar, vanilla and milk. Frost cookies. **Yield:** 2 dozen.

SECRET KISS COOKIES
Karen Owen, Rising Sun, Indiana

Here's a recipe that's literally sealed with a "kiss". This cookie's bound to tickle any sweet tooth.

     1 cup butter (no substitutes), softened
  1/2 cup sugar
     1 teaspoon vanilla extract
     2 cups all-purpose flour
     1 cup finely chopped walnuts
     1 package (8 ounces) milk chocolate kisses
1-1/3 cups confectioners' sugar, *divided*
     2 tablespoons baking cocoa

In a mixing bowl, cream butter, sugar and vanilla. Gradually add flour. Fold in walnuts. Refrigerate dough for 2-3 hours or until firm. Shape into 1-in. balls. Flatten balls and place a chocolate kiss in the center of each; pinch dough together around kiss. Place 2 in. apart on ungreased baking sheets. Bake at 375° for 12 minutes or until set but not browned. Cool for 1 minute; remove from pans to wire racks. Sift 2/3 cup confectioners' sugar and cocoa. While cookies are still warm, roll half in cocoa mixture and half in remaining confectioners' sugar. Cool completely. Store in an airtight container. **Yield:** about 2-1/2 dozen.

COOKIE COLLECTION. Starting clockwise from top left: Celestial Bars (p. 34), Chocolate Reindeer (p. 34), Chocolate-Tipped Butter Cookies (p. 35), Mocha Cherry Cookies (p. 34) and Italian Horn Cookies (p. 34).

CELESTIAL BARS
Maribeth Gregg, Cable, Ohio
(Pictured on page 32)

My aunt gave me the recipe for these wonderfully nutty bars. With their marbled base, fluffy icing and pretty chocolate glaze, they're the stars of bake sales, cookie gift packs and parties.

    1/2 cup butter (no substitutes), softened
    2 cups packed brown sugar
    1 teaspoon vanilla extract
    1/2 teaspoon almond extract
    3 eggs
    2 cups all-purpose flour
    1/2 teaspoon salt
1-1/2 cups chopped pecans
    2 squares (1 ounce *each*) unsweetened chocolate, melted
ICING:
    1/2 cup butter (no substitutes), softened
    3 cups confectioners' sugar
    3 to 4 tablespoons milk
    1 teaspoon vanilla extract
GLAZE:
    1/2 cup semisweet chocolate chips
    2 teaspoons shortening

In a mixing bowl, cream butter and brown sugar. Add extracts. Add eggs, one at a time, beating well after each addition. Combine flour and salt; add to creamed mixture and mix well. Stir in pecans. Divide batter in half; stir chocolate into one portion. Alternately spoon plain and chocolate batters into a greased 13-in. x 9-in. x 2-in. baking pan. Swirl with a knife (the batter will be thick). Bake at 350° for 16-20 minutes or until a toothpick inserted near the center comes out clean. Cool completely. For icing, cream butter and confectioners' sugar in a mixing bowl. Add milk and vanilla; mix until smooth. Spread over bars. For glaze, melt chocolate chips and shortening in a microwave or double boiler. Drizzle over bars. Let stand until chocolate is completely set before cutting. **Yield:** 4 dozen.

ITALIAN HORN COOKIES
Gloria Siddiqui, Houston, Texas
(Pictured on page 32)

My family has been making these delicate fruit-filled Christmas cookies for generations. Light and flaky, they have the look of elegant pastry.

    1 cup cold butter (no substitutes)
    4 cups all-purpose flour
    2 cups vanilla ice cream, softened
    1 can (12-1/2 ounces) cherry filling*
Sugar

In a large bowl, cut butter into flour until mixture resembles coarse crumbs. Stir in ice cream. Divide into four portions. Cover and refrigerate for 2 hours. On a lightly floured surface, roll each portion to 1/8-in. thickness. With a fluted pastry cutter, cut into 2-in. squares. Place about 1/2 teaspoon filling in the center of each square. Overlap two opposite corners of dough over the filling and seal. Sprinkle lightly with sugar. Place on ungreased baking sheets. Bake at 350° for 10-12

minutes or until bottoms are light brown. Cool on wire racks. **Yield:** about 5 dozen. ***Editor's Note:** This recipe was tested using Solo brand cherry filling, found in the baking aisle of most grocery stores. Poppy seed filling may also be used.

CHOCOLATE REINDEER
Lisa Rupple, Keenesburg, Colorado
(Pictured on pages 32 and 33)

These cute cutout reindeer really fly off the plate when my brother's around. They're his favorite! The subtle chocolate color and taste make them a nice alternative to plain vanilla sugar cookies.

    1 cup butter (no substitutes), softened
    1 cup sugar
    1/2 cup packed brown sugar
    1 egg
    1 teaspoon vanilla extract
2-3/4 cups all-purpose flour
    1/2 cup baking cocoa
    1 teaspoon baking soda
    44 red-hot candies
ICING (optional):
1-1/2 cups confectioners' sugar
    2 to 3 tablespoons milk

In a mixing bowl, cream butter and sugars until fluffy. Beat in egg and vanilla. Combine flour, cocoa and baking soda; add to creamed mixture and mix well. Cover and refrigerate for at least 2 hours. On a lightly floured surface, roll dough to 1/8-in. thickness. Cut with a reindeer-shaped cookie cutter. Place on greased baking sheets. Bake at 375° for 8-9 minutes. Immediately press a red-hot onto each nose. Cool for 2-3 minutes; remove from pans to wire racks. If desired, combine confectioners' sugar and milk until smooth. Cut a small hole in the corner of a heavy-duty resealable plastic bag; fill with icing. Pipe around edges of cookies and add a dot for eye. **Yield:** about 3-1/2 dozen.

MOCHA CHERRY COOKIES
Diane Molbert, Emerald Park, Saskatchewan
(Pictured on pages 32 and 33)

Flecked with cherries and glistening with sugar, these dainty cookies always go over big. They're rich and tender, much like shortbread, and have a pleasant chocolate-coffee flavor.

    1 cup butter (no substitutes), softened
    1/2 cup sugar
    1 teaspoon vanilla extract
    1 teaspoon instant coffee granules
    1 teaspoon hot water
    1/4 cup baking cocoa
    2 cups all-purpose flour
    1/2 cup chopped maraschino cherries
    1/2 cup chopped walnuts
Additional sugar
Melted semisweet chocolate, optional

In a mixing bowl, cream butter and sugar until fluffy. Add vanilla. Dissolve coffee granules in water; add to creamed mixture with cocoa. Add flour and mix well. Stir in cherries and walnuts. Shape into 1-1/4-in. balls; roll in sugar. Place on ungreased baking sheets. Bake at 325° for 20-22 minutes. Cool on wire racks. Drizzle with chocolate if desired. **Yield:** about 3 dozen.

CHOCOLATE-TIPPED BUTTER COOKIES
Thara Baker-Alley, Columbia, Missouri
(Pictured on page 33)

My husband and I enjoy these buttery cookies so much that we have a hard time not hiding them from guests!

    1 cup plus 3 tablespoons butter (no substitutes),
        softened, *divided*
1/2 cup confectioners' sugar
    2 cups all-purpose flour
    1 teaspoon vanilla extract
    1 cup (6 ounces) semisweet chocolate chips
1/2 cup finely chopped pecans *or* walnuts

In a mixing bowl, cream 1 cup butter and sugar. Add flour and vanilla; mix well. Cover and refrigerate for 1 hour. Shape 1/2 cupfuls of dough into 1/2-in.-thick logs. Cut logs into 2-1/2-in. pieces; place on ungreased baking sheets. Bake at 350° for 12-14 minutes or until lightly browned. Cool on wire racks. In a microwave or double boiler, melt chocolate and remaining butter. Dip one end of each cookie into chocolate and then into nuts; place on waxed paper until chocolate is set. **Yield:** about 5 dozen.

HONEY SPICE KRINKLES
Donald Shopshire, Salton Sea Beach, California

Sugar and spice make these Christmas cookies among the nicest I've ever tried. Deliciously old-fashioned, they've been our family favorites for years. Busy holiday bakers will be pleased to know that the dough is very easy to work with.

3/4 cup butter (no substitutes), softened
    1 cup packed brown sugar
    1 egg
1/4 cup honey
2-1/4 cups all-purpose flour
1-1/2 teaspoons baking soda
    1 teaspoon ground ginger
1/2 teaspoon salt
1/2 teaspoon ground cinnamon
1/4 teaspoon ground cloves
Sugar

In a mixing bowl, cream butter and brown sugar until fluffy. Beat in egg and honey. Combine flour, baking soda, ginger, salt, cinnamon and cloves; gradually add to creamed mixture and mix well. Cover and refrigerate for at least 2 hours. Shape into 1-in. balls. Dip half of each ball into water and then into sugar. Place with sugar side up 2 in. apart on ungreased baking sheets. Bake at 350° for 15-17 minutes or until lightly browned. Cool on wire racks. **Yield:** about 5 dozen.

ORANGE CRISPIES
Ruth Gladstone, Brunswick, Maryland

When I want to drop a little sunshine into my cookie jar, I bake up a double batch of these citrusy and sweet treats.

    1 cup shortening
    1 cup sugar
    1 egg
1-1/2 teaspoons orange extract
1/2 teaspoon salt
1-1/2 cups flour
Sugar *or* orange-colored sugar

In a mixing bowl, cream shortening and sugar until fluffy. Beat in egg, extract and salt. Add flour; mix well. Drop rounded tablespoonfuls of dough 2 in. apart onto ungreased baking sheets. Bake at 375° for 10 minutes or until edges begin to brown. Cool for 1-2 minutes; remove from pans to wire racks. Sprinkle with sugar while warm. **Yield:** 3-1/2 dozen.

MARZIPAN BARS
Jeanne Koniuszy, Nome, Texas

My husband's grandmother made these lovely layered bars for us as our newlywed Christmas present.

1/2 cup butter (no substitutes), softened
1/2 cup packed brown sugar
    1 egg yolk
    1 teaspoon vanilla extract
    2 cups all-purpose flour
1/2 teaspoon baking soda
1/4 teaspoon salt
1/4 cup milk
    1 jar (10 ounces) raspberry jelly
FILLING:
    1 can (8 ounces) almond paste, cubed
    3 tablespoons butter (no substitutes), softened
1/2 cup sugar
    1 egg white
    1 teaspoon vanilla extract
    3 eggs
    6 drops green food coloring
ICING:
    2 squares (1 ounce *each*) unsweetened chocolate
    1 tablespoon butter (no substitutes)
    2 cups confectioners' sugar
    4 to 5 tablespoons milk
    1 teaspoon vanilla extract

In a mixing bowl, cream butter and brown sugar. Add egg yolk and vanilla; mix well. Combine flour, baking soda and salt; add to creamed mixture alternately with milk. Press into a greased 15-in. x 10-in. x 1-in. baking pan. Spread with jelly. For filling, combine almond paste, butter, sugar, egg white and vanilla in a mixing bowl. Beat in eggs. Add food coloring; mix well. Pour over jelly layer. Bake at 350° for 35 minutes or until set. Cool on a wire rack. For icing, heat chocolate and butter in a small saucepan on low until melted. Add confectioners' sugar and enough milk to make a smooth icing. Stir in vanilla. Immediately spread over bars. Cover and store overnight at room temperature before cutting. **Yield:** about 6-1/2 dozen.

SWEET TREATS! From top to bottom: Popcorn Almond Brittle (p. 37), Napoleon Cremes (p. 37), Truffle Cups (p. 37) and Holiday Wreath (p. 37).

Seasonal Sweets

POPCORN ALMOND BRITTLE
Ruth Peterson, Jenison, Michigan
(Pictured on page 36)

For a crunchy snack that suits the season, try this one. I've been stirring up batches of the distinctive brittle since 1975. With popcorn, almonds and candied cherries tossed together in a sweet crisp coating, it's a festive favorite we enjoy every year.

    6 cups popped popcorn
    1 cup slivered almonds
  1/2 cup *each* red and green candied cherries, chopped
1-1/2 cups sugar
  1/2 cup corn syrup
  1/2 cup water
  1/2 teaspoon salt
    2 tablespoons butter *or* margarine
    1 teaspoon vanilla extract

In a greased 13-in. x 9-in. x 2-in. baking pan, combine popcorn, almonds and cherries. Bake at 350° for 10 minutes. Turn oven off and keep mixture warm in the oven. Meanwhile, in a large heavy saucepan, combine the sugar, corn syrup, water and salt; cook and stir over low heat until sugar is dissolved. Cook over medium heat, without stirring, until a candy thermometer reads 305°-310° (hard-crack stage). Remove from the heat; stir in butter and vanilla. Immediately pour over popcorn mixture; toss gently. Spread onto a greased baking sheet. When cool, break into small pieces. **Yield:** about 1-1/2 pounds.

NAPOLEON CREMES
Gloria Jesswein, Niles, Michigan
(Pictured on page 36)

For the annual Christmas open house we host, I set out a buffet with lots of food and candies like these lovely layered treats. They're so creamy…and with a green pistachio layer of pudding peeking out, they're very merry.

    1 cup butter *or* margarine, softened, *divided*
1/4 cup sugar
1/4 cup baking cocoa
    1 teaspoon vanilla extract
    1 egg, lightly beaten
    2 cups finely crushed graham cracker crumbs
      (about 32 squares)
    1 cup flaked coconut
    3 tablespoons milk
    1 package (3.4 ounces) instant pistachio *or* lemon
      pudding mix
    2 cups confectioners' sugar
TOPPING:
    1 cup (6 ounces) semisweet chocolate chips
    3 tablespoons butter *or* margarine

In a double boiler, combine 1/2 cup butter, sugar, cocoa and vanilla; cook and stir until butter is melted. Add egg; cook and stir until mixture thickens, about 5 minutes. Stir

in crumbs and coconut. Press into a greased 9-in. square baking pan. In a mixing bowl, cream remaining butter. Add milk, pudding mix and confectioners' sugar; beat until fluffy. Spread over crust. Refrigerate until firm, 1-1/2 to 2 hours. Melt chocolate chips and butter; cool. Spread over pudding layer. Refrigerate. Cut into bars. **Yield:** 4 dozen.

TRUFFLE CUPS
Katie Dowler, Birch Tree, Missouri
(Pictured on page 36)

When I serve this elegant confection for the holidays, it never fails to draw compliments. Delightfully tempting, the cups are a fun fluffy variation on traditional truffles.

    1 package (11-1/2 ounces) milk chocolate chips
    2 tablespoons shortening
    1 pound white confectionery coating, cut into
      1/2-inch pieces
  1/2 cup whipping cream

In a double boiler or microwave, melt chips and shortening. Stir until smooth; cool for 5 minutes. With a narrow pastry brush, "paint" the chocolate mixture on the inside of 1-in. foil candy cups. Place on a tray and refrigerate until firm, about 45 minutes. Remove about 12 cups at a time from the refrigerator; remove and discard foil cups. Return chocolate cups to the refrigerator. For filling, melt confectionery coating and cream; stir until smooth. Transfer to a mixing bowl; cover and refrigerate for 30 minutes or until mixture begins to thicken. Beat filling for 1-2 minutes or until light and fluffy. Use a pastry star tube or spoon to fill the chocolate cups. Store in the refrigerator. **Yield:** 5 dozen.

HOLIDAY WREATH
Denise Glisson, Kingshill, U.S. Virgin Islands
(Pictured on page 36)

My mom gave me this recipe. I look forward to crafting and sharing the wreath every Christmas. It's crisp and chewy, and a real eye-catcher on the table.

  30 large marshmallows
 1/2 cup butter (no substitutes)
    1 tablespoon vanilla extract
  20 to 22 drops green food coloring
3-1/2 cups cornflakes
Red-hot candies
Red shoestring licorice and one red Dot candy, optional

In a heavy saucepan, combine marshmallows, butter, vanilla and food coloring; cook and stir over low heat until smooth. Remove from the heat; add cornflakes and mix well. Drop by spoonfuls onto greased foil, forming a 9-in. wreath. Decorate with red-hots. If desired, form a bow with licorice and place on wreath; add Dot on top of bow. **Yield:** 10-12 servings.

CHOCOLATE PEANUT CLUSTERS
Darlyne Shoemaker, Byron Center, Michigan

There are a few recipes I absolutely have to pull out every Christmas, and this is one of them. The nutty clusters are so smooth and chocolaty.

> 2 pounds white confectionery coating
> 1 package (12 ounces) semisweet chocolate chips
> 1 package (11-1/2 ounces) milk chocolate chips
> 5 cups salted dry roasted peanuts

In a heavy saucepan over low heat, cook and stir confectionery coating and chips until melted and smooth. Cool for 10 minutes; stir in peanuts. Drop by rounded tablespoonfuls onto waxed paper-lined baking sheets. Refrigerate until firm, about 45 minutes. **Yield:** 10 dozen.

CARAMEL MARSHMALLOW BUTTONS
Mrs. Terry Dorale, Cody, Wyoming

Kids of all ages dive into these sweet fluffy treats. The chewy marshmallow, gooey caramel and crisp coating set off an appetizing explosion of textures.

> 50 to 54 large marshmallows
> 1 package (14 ounces) caramels
> 1 can (14 ounces) sweetened condensed milk
> 1 cup butter *or* margarine
> 5 to 6 cups crisp rice cereal

Place a toothpick in each marshmallow. Place on waxed paper-lined baking sheets. Freeze until firm, about 1 hour. In a heavy saucepan over medium-low heat, combine caramels, milk and butter. Cook and stir until caramels are melted and mixture is smooth. Dip marshmallows in caramel mixture; roll in cereal. Freeze until firm, at least 1 hour. Remove from the freezer 45 minutes before serving; discard toothpicks. **Yield:** 50-54 pieces.

DATE NUT CANDY
Pauline Block, Aurora, Indiana

Even though my two grown sons aren't big "sweets eaters", they think these candies are exceptional. The big peanut butter flavor is a hit combined with holiday staples like walnuts and dates.

> 1 cup creamy peanut butter
> 1 cup confectioners' sugar
> 1 cup chopped dates
> 1 cup chopped walnuts
> 1 tablespoon butter *or* margarine, softened
> 1 teaspoon vanilla extract
> 1 pound white confectionery coating

In a mixing bowl, combine the first six ingredients; mix well. Shape into 3/4-in. balls; place on a waxed paper-lined baking sheet. Refrigerate for 1-2 hours or until firm. In a microwave or double boiler, melt confectionery coating; stir until smooth. Dip balls in coating and place on waxed paper to harden. **Yield:** about 4 dozen.

CHEWY CHOCOLATE LOGS
Pat Walter, Pine Island, Minnesota

When I made these for our church Christmas bazaar, folks would snap them up within minutes. They're nice and soft like chocolate caramels but not sticky.

> 2 squares (1 ounce *each*) unsweetened baking chocolate
> 2 tablespoons butter *or* margarine
> 1/2 cup light corn syrup
> 1 teaspoon vanilla extract
> 3 cups confectioners' sugar, *divided*
> 3/4 cup instant nonfat dry milk powder

In a saucepan over low heat, melt chocolate and butter. Transfer to a mixing bowl; add corn syrup, vanilla, 2 cups confectioners' sugar and milk powder. Mix well. Place remaining sugar on a clean surface; place dough on the surface and knead sugar into the dough until all of it is absorbed. Shape teaspoonfuls into 2-in. logs; wrap in waxed paper and twist ends. Refrigerate until firm. **Yield:** about 6 dozen.

MARBLED ALMOND ROCA
Niki-Jeanne Rooke, Pollockville, Alberta

My easy recipe is an old favorite that we keep in steady use from mid-November until the New Year. Homemade gifts are still a Christmas tradition at our house.

> 1/2 cup slivered almonds
> 1 cup butter *or* margarine
> 1 cup sugar
> 3 tablespoons boiling water
> 2 tablespoons light corn syrup
> 1/2 cup semisweet chocolate chips
> 1/2 cup vanilla baking chips

Sprinkle almonds on a greased 15-in. x 10-in. x 1-in. baking pan. Bake at 300° for 15 minutes or until toasted and golden brown; remove from the oven and set aside. In a saucepan over low heat, cook butter and sugar for 5 minutes. Add water and corn syrup. Bring to a boil over medium heat; cook, stirring occasionally, until a candy thermometer reads 300° (hard-crack stage). Quickly pour over almonds. Sprinkle chips on top; let stand for 1-2 minutes or until melted. Spread and swirl chocolate over candy. Cool completely; break into pieces. **Yield:** 1-1/2 pounds.

HOLIDAY DIVINITY
Helen White, Kerrville, Texas

I've been whipping up this Christmasy treat—with its jolly red and green candied cherries and scrumptious chopped nuts—since 1955. It's so light it melts in your mouth.

> 2 cups sugar
> 1/2 cup water
> 1/3 cup light corn syrup
> 2 egg whites
> 1 teaspoon vanilla extract
> 1/8 teaspoon salt

1/4 cup diced candied cherries
1/4 cup diced candied pineapple
1 cup chopped walnuts

In a heavy saucepan, combine sugar, water and corn syrup; cook and stir until sugar is dissolved and mixture comes to a boil. Cook over medium heat, without stirring, until a candy thermometer reads 250° (hard-ball stage). Remove from the heat. In a mixing bowl, beat the egg whites until stiff peaks form. Slowly pour hot sugar mixture over egg whites, beating constantly. Add vanilla and salt. Beat until candy loses its gloss and holds its shape, about 14 minutes. Stir in fruit and nuts. Drop by teaspoonfuls onto waxed paper. **Yield:** 1-1/4 pounds. **Editor's Note:** The use of a hand mixer is not recommended for this recipe.

PEANUT BUTTER TRUFFLES
Kim Barker, Richmond, Texas

Crunchy granola provides a surprising texture that brings raves when people sample these yummy peanut butter truffles.

    5 ounces white confectionery coating, *divided*
    2/3 cup creamy peanut butter
    1/2 cup confectioners' sugar
    1 tablespoon vanilla extract
    2/3 cup crushed granola cereal with oats and honey
    6 squares (1 ounce *each*) semisweet chocolate
    2 tablespoons shortening

In a microwave or double boiler, melt 3 ounces white confectionery coating. Stir in peanut butter until smooth. Add sugar, vanilla and cereal. Shape into 1-in. balls; set aside. Melt chocolate and shortening; dip balls and place on a wire rack over waxed paper. Let stand for 15 minutes or until firm. Melt the remaining coating; cool for 5 minutes. Drizzle over truffles. Chill for 5-10 minutes or until firm. Cover and store in the refrigerator. **Yield:** 3 dozen.

CHOCOLATE CINNAMON MUD BALLS
Marlene Gates, Bozeman, Montana

A friend's mother who knows I love to cook shared this recipe. These delicious candies won a blue ribbon at our local fair!

    2 cups sugar
    1/2 cup water
    1/4 cup whipping cream
    1 tablespoon light corn syrup
    1-1/2 squares (1-1/2 ounces) semisweet baking
        chocolate, chopped
    1 to 2 teaspoons ground cinnamon
    1 teaspoon vanilla extract
Pinch salt
    2-1/2 cups (15 ounces) semisweet chocolate chips
    1 tablespoon shortening
    1/2 cup ground nuts, optional

Butter the sides of a heavy saucepan; add the first five ingredients. Cook and stir over medium-high heat until sugar is dissolved. Cook, without stirring, until a candy thermometer reads 238° (soft-ball stage). Remove from the heat. Cool, without stirring, until mixture reaches 110°. Transfer to a mixing bowl; add cinnamon, vanilla and salt. Beat until light-colored and stiff enough to knead, about 2 minutes. Lightly grease hands; knead mixture in bowl for 2 minutes or until smooth. Roll into 1-in. balls; cover and freeze for 20 minutes. Melt chips and shortening; dip the balls, shaking off excess. Roll in nuts if desired. Place on waxed paper-lined baking sheets to harden. **Yield:** 3 dozen.

MIXED NUT BRITTLE
Mrs. James Merriman, Preble, Indiana

Peanut brittle is done one better when prepared with mixed nuts instead. This impressive candy is simply delicious. I like to pack some in pretty plastic bags to give as gifts.

    4 cups mixed nuts
    1-1/2 cups sugar
    1 cup light corn syrup
    1/3 cup water
    2 tablespoons butter *or* margarine
    1 teaspoon vanilla extract
    1/2 teaspoon salt

Place nuts in two greased 15-in. x 10-in. x 1-in. baking pans. Bake at 350° for 10 minutes or until warm. Set aside and keep warm. Meanwhile, in a large heavy saucepan, combine sugar, corn syrup and water. Cover and bring to a boil over medium heat. Uncover and cook until a candy thermometer reads 290° (soft-crack stage). Remove from the heat; stir in nuts, butter, vanilla and salt. Quickly spread into a thin layer on baking pans. Cool completely; break into pieces. **Yield:** 2-1/2 pounds.

ANGEL FOOD CANDY
Carrol Holloway, Hindsville, Arkansas

Dipped in both white and dark chocolate, this two-toned candy really stands out on the goody tray. A batch is a tasty gift as well.

    1 cup sugar
    1 cup dark corn syrup
    1 tablespoon vinegar
    1 tablespoon baking soda
    1/2 pound white confectionery coating
    1/2 pound dark chocolate confectionery coating

In a large heavy saucepan, combine sugar, corn syrup and vinegar. Cook and stir over medium heat until sugar is dissolved. Cook, without stirring, until a candy thermometer reads 290° (soft-crack stage). Remove from the heat; stir in baking soda. Pour into a buttered 13-in. x 9-in. x 2-in. pan. Cool. Break into pieces. Melt white confectionery coating; dip the candies halfway, shaking off excess. Place on waxed paper-lined baking sheets to harden. Melt dark chocolate coating; dip uncoated portion of candies. Return to waxed paper to harden. **Yield:** 1-1/2 pounds.

● Confectionery coating, sometimes labeled "almond bark" or "candy coating", is found in the baking section of most grocery stores. It is often sold in bulk packages of 1 to 1-1/2 pounds. Used for dipping chocolate, it is available in white, milk and dark chocolate varieties.

DAZZLING DESSERTS! Top to bottom: Confetti Cream Cake (p. 41), Christmas Cheesecake (p. 41) and Lady Lamington Cakes (p. 41).

Festive Desserts

CHRISTMAS CHEESECAKE
Verna Arthur, Perkins, Oklahoma
(Pictured on page 40)

With a cheery cherry topping and mint green garnish, this is the perfect dessert to top off a holiday dinner.

1-1/2 cups graham cracker crumbs (about 24 squares)
    6 tablespoons butter *or* margarine, melted
    1 envelope unflavored gelatin
1/4 cup cold water
1/4 cup milk
    1 package (8 ounces) cream cheese, softened
1/2 cup confectioners' sugar
    2 teaspoons grated lemon peel
    1 carton (8 ounces) frozen whipped topping, thawed, *divided*
    1 can (21 ounces) cherry pie filling

Combine crumbs and butter; press onto the bottom of a greased 9-in. springform pan. Chill 15 minutes. In a saucepan, combine gelatin and water; let stand for 1 minute. Add milk; cook and stir over low heat until gelatin is dissolved. Beat cream cheese and sugar until light and fluffy. Add gelatin mixture and lemon peel; mix well. Chill until partially set. Fold in 2 cups whipped topping. Pour over crust. Chill until firm, at least 3 hours. Spread pie filling over gelatin layer. Top with remaining whipped topping. **Yield:** 10-12 servings.

CONFETTI CREAM CAKE
Jennie Moshier, Fresno, California
(Pictured on page 40)

Luscious layers of cake and creamy filling form this eye-popping dessert. If you're short on time, ready the filling ingredients a day ahead. Then assemble and frost right before serving.

    5 eggs
    1 teaspoon vanilla extract
    1 cup sugar
    1 cup all-purpose flour
1/2 teaspoon baking powder
1/2 teaspoon salt
FILLING:
    1 package (8 ounces) cream cheese, softened
    1 cup sugar, *divided*
    1 teaspoon vanilla extract
1/4 teaspoon ground cinnamon
    1 cup (8 ounces) sour cream
1/2 cup finely chopped walnuts
1/2 cup flaked coconut, optional
1/3 cup chopped maraschino cherries
    2 milk chocolate candy bars (1.55 ounces *each*), shaved *or* finely chopped
1-1/2 cups whipping cream

In a mixing bowl, beat eggs and vanilla on high until foamy. Add sugar; beat until thick and lemon-colored. Combine flour, baking powder and salt; fold into egg mixture, a third

at a time. Pour into two greased and floured 9-in. round baking pans. Bake at 350° for 25-30 minutes or until cake springs back when lightly touched. Cool for 5 minutes; remove from pans to wire racks to cool completely. In a mixing bowl, beat cream cheese, 2/3 cup sugar, vanilla and cinnamon until smooth. Stir in sour cream, nuts, coconut and cherries. Fold in chocolate. Beat cream and remaining sugar; set half aside. Fold remaining whipped cream into the cream cheese mixture. Split each cake into two horizontal layers; spread a fourth of the cream cheese mixture on one layer. Repeat layers. Frost sides with reserved whipped cream. Refrigerate until serving. **Yield:** 10-12 servings.

LADY LAMINGTON CAKES
Dee Pufpaff, Raleigh, North Carolina
(Pictured on page 40)

I learned to turn out these dainty no-bake cakes while living in Australia. Named for the wife of a past governor from "down under", they make a lip-smacking snack or dessert.

    1 package (10-3/4 ounces) frozen pound cake
1/3 cup water
    2 tablespoons butter *or* margarine
1/4 cup baking cocoa
2-1/2 cups confectioners' sugar
    4 cups shredded coconut, toasted and chopped

Thaw cake; cut into 3/4-in. slices. Cut each slice into four fingers; set aside. In a microwave-safe bowl or saucepan, heat water and butter until butter is melted. Whisk in cocoa until dissolved. Whisk in sugar to make a thin glaze. Dip cakes into glaze to coat all sides; roll in coconut. Place on waxed paper to dry. Cover and refrigerate. **Yield:** 3 dozen.

CRANBERRY CREAM
Sharlene Atkinson, Tacoma, Washington

This delightful gelatin cream brings Christmas meals to a happy ending. It's not heavy, and I relish its zesty goodness.

2-1/2 cups orange juice, *divided*
    1 can (16 ounces) jellied cranberry sauce
    1 package (6 ounces) raspberry gelatin
1-1/2 cups whipping cream
    1 to 2 medium oranges, peeled and sectioned
  1/4 cup fresh *or* frozen cranberries, thawed
Corn syrup and sugar

In a saucepan, combine 3/4 cup orange juice, cranberry sauce and gelatin. Mash and cook over medium-low heat until gelatin is dissolved. Stir in remaining orange juice. Chill until mixture begins to thicken, about 2-1/2 hours. Beat cream until soft peaks form; fold into gelatin mixture. Pour into an 8-cup serving bowl; refrigerate until firm. Garnish with oranges. Brush cranberries with corn syrup; sprinkle with sugar. Place over oranges. **Yield:** 8-10 servings.

RASPBERRY WALNUT TORTE
Helen Schmidt, Moline, Illinois

I get lots of compliments on this sweet treat filled with nuts and fruity flavor. It was a favorite at the tearoom I once operated.

    1/2 cup butter *or* margarine, softened
    1/3 cup sugar
    1 egg
1-1/4 cups all-purpose flour
    1 cup ground walnuts
    1 jar (12 ounces) raspberry preserves, *divided*
FILLING:
    4 eggs
    3/4 cup packed brown sugar
    2 cups flaked coconut
    2 cups chopped walnuts
    2 tablespoons all-purpose flour
    1/4 teaspoon baking powder
    2 to 3 tablespoons water

In a mixing bowl, cream butter and sugar. Add egg; mix well. Add flour; mix until blended. Stir in walnuts. Press onto the bottom and 1-1/2 in. up the sides of a greased 9-in. springform pan. Refrigerate for 1 hour. Spread 1/4 cup preserves over crust. In a mixing bowl, beat eggs and brown sugar until light and fluffy. Combine coconut, walnuts, flour and baking powder; fold into egg mixture. Pour into crust. Bake at 350° for 1 hour. Cool; remove sides of pan. Thin remaining preserves with water. Spread over torte. **Yield:** 10-12 servings.

EGGNOG POUND CAKE
Theresa Koetter, Borden, Indiana

A flavorful blend of eggnog and nutmeg makes this cake a natural holiday favorite. It uses a convenient boxed mix base.

    1 package (18-1/4 ounces) yellow cake mix
    1 cup eggnog*
    3 eggs
    1/2 cup butter *or* margarine, softened
    1/2 to 1 teaspoon ground nutmeg
CUSTARD SAUCE:
    1/4 cup sugar
    1 tablespoon cornstarch
    1/4 teaspoon salt
    1 cup milk
    1 egg yolk, lightly beaten
    1 teaspoon butter *or* margarine
    1 teaspoon vanilla extract
    1/2 cup whipping cream, whipped

In a mixing bowl, combine the first five ingredients. Beat on low until moistened, scraping bowl occasionally. Beat on medium for 2 minutes. Pour into a greased and floured 12-cup fluted tube pan. Bake at 350° for 40-45 minutes or until a toothpick inserted near the center comes out clean. Cool in pan for 10 minutes; invert onto a wire rack. Remove from pan; cool completely. For sauce, combine sugar, cornstarch and salt in a saucepan; gradually stir in milk. Bring to a boil over medium heat; boil for 1-2 minutes, stirring constantly. Blend a small amount into egg yolk. Return all to the pan; mix well. Cook and stir for 2 minutes. Remove from the heat; stir in butter and vanilla. Cool for 15 minutes. Fold in whipped cream. Store in the refrigerator. Serve with the cake. **Yield:** 16-20 servings. *Editor's Note:* This recipe was tested with commercially prepared eggnog.

PEPPERMINT CHARLOTTE
Lucille Watters, Palmyra, Missouri

My guests always save room for this pretty pink peppermint dessert. You'll know why after just one cool and fluffy bite.

    2 envelopes unflavored gelatin
3-1/2 cups milk
    1/2 cup sugar
    1/8 teaspoon salt
    5 egg yolks, beaten
    1/2 cup finely crushed peppermint candy
    8 drops red food coloring
1-1/2 cups whipping cream, whipped
    12 ladyfingers, split

In a saucepan, soften gelatin in milk for 1 minute. Stir in sugar and salt. Cook and stir over medium-low heat for 5 minutes or until gelatin is dissolved. Remove from the heat. Stir a small amount of hot mixture into egg yolks. Return all to the pan. Cook and stir over low heat until the mixture thickens slightly and coats the back of a metal spoon or reaches 160° (do not boil). Remove from the heat. Add candy and food coloring; stir until candy is dissolved. Refrigerate, stirring occasionally, until mixture begins to thicken, about 30 minutes. Fold in whipped cream. Place ladyfinger halves around a greased 9-in. springform pan. Pour mixture into center of pan. Cover and chill for 4 hours or overnight. Just before serving, run a knife around edge of pan to loosen; remove sides. **Yield:** 10-12 servings.

OLD-FASHIONED CHOCOLATE PIE
Betsey Sue Halcott, Lebanon, Connecticut

Preparing this old-fashioned pie brings back memories. When I was a girl, we cranked homemade ice cream to serve with it.

    1/2 cup water
1-1/2 squares (1-1/2 ounces) unsweetened baking
       chocolate
    1/4 cup butter *or* margarine
    2/3 cup sugar
1-1/2 teaspoons vanilla extract
FILLING:
    1/4 cup shortening
    3/4 cup sugar
    1 egg
    1 cup all-purpose flour
    1 teaspoon baking powder
    1/2 teaspoon salt
    1/2 cup milk
    1 unbaked pastry shell (9 inches)
    2 tablespoons chopped nuts, optional

In a saucepan, bring water, chocolate and butter to a boil; boil for 1 minute. Remove from the heat; add sugar and vanilla. Set aside. In a mixing bowl, cream shortening and sugar until light and fluffy. Add egg; beat well. Combine flour, baking powder and salt; add to creamed mixture alternately with milk. Pour pastry shell. Carefully pour reserved chocolate mixture over filling. Sprinkle with nuts if desired. Cover edges of pastry with foil. Bake at 350° for 55-60 minutes or until a toothpick inserted near the center comes out clean. **Yield:** 8 servings.

ELIZABETH'S PUMPKIN PIE
Elizabeth Montgomery, Taylorville, Illinois

In my ice cream-loving husband's opinion, traditional pumpkin pie can't compare with this melt-in-your-mouth version.

```
    1 quart vanilla ice cream, softened
    1 pastry shell (9 inches), baked
    1 cup canned or cooked pumpkin
3/4 cup sugar
1/2 teaspoon ground cinnamon
1/2 teaspoon salt
Dash ground nutmeg
    1 cup whipping cream, whipped
SYRUP:
1/2 cup packed brown sugar
1/4 cup water
1/4 cup dark corn syrup
1/4 teaspoon vanilla extract
1/8 teaspoon almond extract
```

Spread ice cream into pastry shell. Cover and freeze until firm. In a bowl, combine pumpkin, sugar, cinnamon, salt and nutmeg; fold in whipped cream. Pour evenly over ice cream; cover and freeze until firm. For syrup, combine brown sugar, water and corn syrup in a saucepan; bring to a boil. Boil for 4-5 minutes, stirring often. Cool; stir in extracts. Drizzle over pie. **Yield:** 6-8 servings.

CHOCOLATE MOUSSE LOAF
Daphene Miller, Princeton, Missouri

This showstopping loaf would make a tempting centerpiece for the most sumptuous holiday table.

```
    2 cups whipping cream, divided
    3 egg yolks
   16 squares (1 ounce each) semisweet baking
      chocolate
1/2 cup butter or margarine
1/2 cup light corn syrup
1/4 cup confectioners' sugar
    1 teaspoon vanilla extract
RASPBERRY SAUCE:
    1 package (10 ounces) frozen raspberries, thawed
1/4 cup light corn syrup
```

In a bowl, whisk 1/2 cup whipping cream and egg yolks; set aside. In a 3-qt. saucepan, heat chocolate, butter and corn syrup over low heat until chocolate and butter are melted. Remove from the heat. Stir about 1 cup into the egg yolk mixture; return all to the pan. Cook and stir over low heat until mixture coats the back of a metal spoon or reaches 160°. Remove from the heat; cool. In a mixing bowl, beat

remaining cream with confectioners' sugar and vanilla until soft peaks form. Fold into chocolate mixture until well blended. Pour into a 9-in. x 5-in. x 3-in. loaf pan that has been lined with plastic wrap. Refrigerate for 8-10 hours. For sauce, place raspberries in a blender; cover and puree. Strain and discard seeds. Stir corn syrup into raspberry puree; refrigerate. Unmold mousse onto a serving platter; serve with raspberry sauce. **Yield:** 12-14 servings.

CRANBERRY APPLE-NUT PIE
Peggy Burdick, Burlington, Michigan

Wedges of this tangy Christmas-red pie are a feast for the eyes and the taste buds.

```
    2 cups fresh or frozen cranberries, chopped
1-3/4 cups sliced peeled tart apple
1/2 cup slivered almonds, toasted
    1 tablespoon grated orange peel
1-3/4 cups sugar
1/4 cup all-purpose flour
1/2 teaspoon ground cinnamon
1/2 teaspoon ground nutmeg
1/8 teaspoon salt
Pastry for double-crust pie (9 inches)
    2 tablespoons butter or margarine, melted
```

In a large bowl, combine cranberries, apple, almonds and orange peel. In another bowl, combine sugar, flour, cinnamon, nutmeg and salt; add to fruit mixture and toss gently. Line a 9-in. pie plate with the bottom crust; add filling. Drizzle with butter. Roll out remaining pastry to fit top of pie. Place over filling; cut slits in top crust. Seal and flute edges. Bake at 400° for 45 minutes or until golden brown. Cool before serving. **Yield:** 6-8 servings.

BLACK FOREST CHEESECAKES
Jean Olson, Wallingford, Iowa

As sure as chocolate and cherries go together, so do my family's Yuletides and these no-fuss cheesecakes.

```
   12 cream-filled chocolate sandwich cookies
    2 packages (8 ounces each) cream cheese, softened
3/4 cup sugar
1/3 cup baking cocoa
    1 teaspoon vanilla extract
    2 eggs
    1 can (21 ounces) cherry pie filling
1/2 to 1 cup whipped topping
```

Remove cookie top from each sandwich cookie; crush and set aside. Place cream-topped cookies in foil-lined muffin cups, cream side up. In a mixing bowl, beat cream cheese, sugar, cocoa and vanilla until fluffy. Beat in eggs until blended. Fill muffin cups three-fourths full. Sprinkle 1/4 cup reserved cookie crumbs over tops (discard remaining crumbs or save for another use). Bake at 325° for 20-25 minutes or until set. Cool completely. Cover and refrigerate for at least 2 hours. Just before serving, top each cheesecake with about 2 tablespoons of pie filling. Top with a dollop of whipped topping. **Yield:** 12 servings.

GIFT-WRAPPED GOODIES! Clockwise from top left: Butterscotch Dip (p. 45), Candy Apple Jelly (p. 45), Hidden Mint Morsels (p. 45) and Coffee Stirrer Sticks (p. 45).

Gifts from the Kitchen

BUTTERSCOTCH DIP
Kay Parker, Albany, Georgia
(Pictured on page 44)

This gooey-good dip is an appealing addition to my Yuletide fruit baskets. I just pour some into pint jars trimmed with Christmas ribbons and tuck them in with red and green apples.

  2 cans (14 ounces *each*) sweetened condensed milk
  2 packages (11 ounces *each*) butterscotch chips
  2 tablespoons vinegar
  1 tablespoon ground cinnamon
Apple slices

In a heavy saucepan over low heat, combine milk, chips, vinegar and cinnamon. Cook and stir until smooth. Serve warm with apples. Leftover sauce may be reheated in a heavy saucepan over low heat. **Yield:** about 4 cups.

CANDY APPLE JELLY
Betsy Porter, Bismarck, North Dakota
(Pictured on page 44)

With a hint of apple and cinnamon, this jelly spreads cheer from breads to bagels to muffins. Its rosy pink color looks lovely blushing through the food jars I save and decorate with fabric-covered lids.

  4 cups apple juice
  1/2 cup red-hot candies
  1 package (1-3/4 ounces) powdered fruit pectin
4-1/2 cups sugar

In a large kettle, combine apple juice, candies and pectin. Bring to a full rolling boil over high heat, stirring constantly. Stir in sugar; return to a full rolling boil. Boil for 2 minutes, stirring constantly. Remove from the heat; skim off any foam and undissolved candies. Pour hot liquid into hot jars, leaving 1/4-in. headspace. Adjust caps. Process for 5 minutes in a boiling-water bath. **Yield:** about 6 half-pints.

HIDDEN MINT MORSELS
Adina Skilbred, Prairie du Sac, Wisconsin
(Pictured on page 44)

Is it a cookie or a candy? No matter which answer folks choose, they find these minty morsels yummy. The recipe makes so much that you can whip up dozens of gifts at once.

  1/3 cup shortening
  1/3 cup butter (no substitutes), softened
  3/4 cup sugar
    1 egg
    1 tablespoon milk
    1 teaspoon vanilla extract
1-3/4 cups all-purpose flour
  1/3 cup baking cocoa

  1-1/2 teaspoons baking powder
    1/4 teaspoon salt
    1/8 teaspoon ground cinnamon
PEPPERMINT LAYER:
    4 cups confectioners' sugar
    6 tablespoons light corn syrup
    6 tablespoons butter (no substitutes), melted
    2 to 3 teaspoons peppermint extract
CHOCOLATE COATING:
    2 packages (11-1/2 ounces *each*) milk chocolate chips
    1/4 cup shortening

In a mixing bowl, cream shortening, butter and sugar until light and fluffy. Add egg, milk and vanilla; mix well. Combine flour, cocoa, baking powder, salt and cinnamon; add to the creamed mixture and mix well. Cover and refrigerate for 8 hours or overnight. On a lightly floured surface, roll dough to 1/8-in. thickness. Cut with a 1-1/2-in. round cookie cutter; place on ungreased baking sheets. Bake at 375° for 6-8 minutes or until set. Cool for 2 minutes; remove to wire racks to cool completely. Combine peppermint layer ingredients; mix well. Knead for 1 minute or until smooth. Shape into 120 balls, 1/2 in. each. Place a ball on each cookie and flatten to cover cookie. Place on waxed paper-lined baking sheets; refrigerate for 30 minutes. In a microwave or double boiler, melt chips and shortening. Spread about 1 teaspoonful over each cookie. Chill until firm. **Yield:** about 10 dozen.

COFFEE STIRRER STICKS
Kelly Pickering, Mesa, Arizona
(Pictured on page 44)

As a holiday novelty, it's hard to lick this lollipop for grown-ups! It doubles as a coffee stirrer, and it makes a special party favor or stocking stuffer.

    1 cup sugar
  1/3 cup brewed coffee
    1 tablespoon light corn syrup
  1/4 teaspoon baking cocoa
  1/4 teaspoon ground cinnamon
  1/2 teaspoon vanilla extract
   12 wooden lollipop *or* craft sticks
Plastic wrap
Red and green narrow ribbon

In a saucepan, combine sugar, coffee, corn syrup, cocoa and cinnamon. Cook over medium heat until the sugar is dissolved, stirring constantly. Cook over medium heat, without stirring, until a candy thermometer reads 290° (soft-crack stage), about 7 minutes. Remove from the heat. Immediately stir in vanilla, then pour into a greased 2-cup heat-proof glass measuring cup. Working quickly, pour tablespoonfuls into circles on a greased baking sheet and lay a stick in each circle. Allow to cool until hardened. When cooled, wrap with plastic wrap and tie with ribbon. Store in an airtight container. **Yield:** about 1 dozen.

PEAR MINCEMEAT
Gay Nell Nicholas, Henderson, Texas

At my house, Christmas isn't Christmas without mincemeat. This fruit- and spice-filled version is ideal for gift-giving—along with my recipe for Pear Mincemeat Pie (below).

- 7 pounds pears, peeled and cored
- 1 medium tart unpeeled apple, cored
- 1 lemon, halved and seeded
- 1 pound raisins
- 4 cups sugar
- 1 cup purple grape juice
- 1 cup vinegar
- 1 tablespoon *each* ground cinnamon, cloves and allspice
- 1 teaspoon salt

In a food processor or grinder, chop or grind pears, apple and lemon. Transfer to a large kettle. Add remaining ingredients; simmer for 2 hours, stirring occasionally. Pack hot mixture into hot jars, leaving 1/2-in. headspace. Adjust caps. Process for 25 minutes in a boiling-water bath. **Yield:** about 8 pints.

PEAR MINCEMEAT PIE

- 2 pints Pear Mincemeat (recipe above)
- 3/4 cup packed brown sugar
- 3 tablespoons all-purpose flour
- 3/4 cup chopped pecans
- 3 tablespoons butter *or* margarine
- Pastry for double-crust pie (9 inches)

In a saucepan, combine mincemeat, brown sugar and flour. Bring to a boil; boil for 1 minute. Remove from the heat; add pecans and butter. Line a 9-in. pie plate with bottom crust. Add filling. Roll out remaining pastry to fit top of pie; cut slits in pastry. Place over filling; seal and flute edges. Bake at 350° for 30-40 minutes or until golden brown. Cool completely before slicing. **Yield:** 6-8 servings.

SUSIE'S HOT MUSTARD
Susie Gibson, Alta Loma, California

My husband enjoys spreading this bold, robust mustard on anything that needs an extra "bite" of flavor.

- 1 can (4 ounces) ground mustard
- 1 cup white wine vinegar
- 3 eggs
- 3/4 cup sugar
- 1 tablespoon honey
- 1 tablespoon molasses
- 2 cups mayonnaise
- 1 tablespoon mustard seed, optional

Combine mustard and vinegar in a small bowl. Cover and let stand at room temperature for 8 hours or overnight. In a saucepan, beat eggs. Stir in sugar, honey, molasses and mustard mixture. Cook and stir over low heat until thickened and a thermometer reads 165°, about 20 minutes. Cool. Stir in mayonnaise and mustard seed if desired. Cover and refrigerate for up to 3 weeks. **Yield:** 4 cups.

SPICY PECANS 'N' CRANBERRIES
Rene Dalrymple, Hansville, Washington

Spice up a holiday party with these well-seasoned nuts—or keep a batch in the freezer to give as last-minute presents.

- 2 tablespoons butter *or* margarine, melted
- 2 tablespoons Worcestershire sauce
- 1/2 teaspoon ground cumin
- 1/2 teaspoon garlic powder
- 1/2 teaspoon seasoned salt
- 1/4 to 1/2 teaspoon cayenne pepper
- 3 cups pecan halves
- 1-1/2 cups dried cranberries

Combine the first six ingredients in a large bowl. Add pecans and mix well. Spread in an ungreased 13-in. x 9-in. x 2-in. baking pan. Bake at 350° for 15 minutes, stirring every 5 minutes. Cool completely. Stir in cranberries. Store in an airtight container. **Yield:** about 4 cups.

CHERRY ALMOND MINI LOAVES
Connie Simon, Reed City, Missouri

Plenty of good things come in these little loaves featuring golden raisins and cherries. There's a surprise—the creamy almond filling—in every scrumptious bite.

- 3/4 cup milk
- 3/4 cup butter *or* margarine, *divided*
- 1/2 cup sugar
- 1 teaspoon salt
- 2 packages (1/4 ounce *each*) active dry yeast
- 1/4 cup warm water (110° to 115°)
- 2 eggs plus 1 egg yolk
- 5-1/2 to 6 cups all-purpose flour
- 1-1/2 cups golden raisins
- 1-1/3 cups candied cherry halves
- 1 teaspoon grated orange peel
- FILLING:
- 1 can (8 ounces) almond paste
- 1/2 cup sugar
- 1 egg white
- Confectioners' sugar

In a saucepan, combine milk, 1/2 cup butter, sugar and salt. Cook over low heat until butter is melted. Cool to lukewarm (110°-115°). In a mixing bowl, dissolve yeast in water. Stir in milk mixture, eggs and yolk. Beat in 2 cups flour, raisins, cherries and orange peel. Add enough remaining flour to form a soft dough. Turn onto a floured surface; knead until smooth and elastic, about 6-8 minutes. Place in a greased bowl, turning once to grease top. Cover and let rise in a warm place until doubled, about 1-1/2 hours. For filling, crumble almond paste into a bowl; stir in sugar and egg white until smooth. Punch dough down; divide into 12 portions. Shape each into a 6-in. x 4-in. oval. Place 2 in. apart on greased baking sheets. Melt remaining butter and brush over dough. Divide almond mixture into 12 portions; roll each into a 5-in. log. Flatten slightly and place off-center on ovals. Fold dough over filling; press edges to seal. Cover and let rise until doubled, about 45 minutes. Brush with butter. Bake at 350° for 20 minutes or until golden brown. Dust with confectioners' sugar. **Yield:** 12 mini loaves.

CHRISTMAS SPICE MIX
Gloria Hoesing, O'Neill, Nebraska

Wonderfully versatile, this gift is seasoned for both sipping and sniffing. When mixed with fruit juices, it's a delicious winter warmer-upper. Boiled in water, it makes a "scentsational" potpourri that will add a heavenly fragrance to the whole house!

SPICE MIX:
- 1 cinnamon stick (3 inches)
- 1 teaspoon ground cinnamon
- 1 teaspoon whole allspice
- 1/2 teaspoon whole cloves
- 1/2 teaspoon ground ginger
- 1/4 teaspoon ground nutmeg

ADDITIONAL INGREDIENTS FOR CRANBERRY WASSAIL:
- 1 quart cranberry juice
- 1 quart pineapple juice
- 1/2 cup sugar

Combine spice mix ingredients; place in the center of two 6-in. square pieces of cheesecloth. Bring corners together and tie with string or dental floss. **Yield:** 1 spice bag. **To use as a room scent:** Place spice bag in a 2-cup microwave-safe measuring cup filled with hot water. Microwave on high for 5-6 minutes or until water boils. Continue to microwave at 30% power to add fragrance to the whole house. (Add more water if microwaved for additional time.) **To prepare cranberry wassail:** Combine juices, sugar and spice bag in a 2-qt. microwave-safe bowl. Cover with plastic wrap and cut a vent. Microwave on high for 14 minutes or until mixture boils. Microwave at 50% power 5 minutes longer. **Yield:** 2 quarts. **Editor's Note:** This recipe was tested in a 700-watt microwave.

NO-CANDIED-FRUIT FRUITCAKE
Sally Vest, Palatine, Illinois

Minus the candied fruit, this traditional cake has a positively natural taste. For those who bake their Christmas giveaways ahead, it freezes beautifully, too.

- 1-1/2 cups all-purpose flour
- 1-1/2 cups sugar
- 1 teaspoon baking powder
- 1 teaspoon salt
- 5-1/2 cups pecan halves
- 2 jars (16 ounces *each*) maraschino cherries, drained
- 1 can (20 ounces) crushed pineapple, drained
- 2 packages (8 ounces *each*) pitted dates, halved and quartered
- 6 eggs
- 1/2 cup orange juice
- 1/4 to 1/2 cup corn syrup

In a large bowl, combine the first four ingredients. Add pecans, cherries, pineapple and dates; toss to coat. Beat eggs and orange juice; add to fruit mixture and mix well. Line two 9-in. x 5-in. x 3-in. loaf pans with foil and grease the foil. Pour fruit mixture into pans and press down. Bake at 300° for 1-3/4 to 2 hours or until a toothpick inserted near the center comes out clean. Cool for 10 minutes; remove from pans. Remove foil. Brush with corn syrup; cool completely. **Yield:** 2 fruitcakes.

RED BEANS AND RICE MIX
Trudie Hagen, Roggen, Colorado

Since there's food galore during the holidays themselves, I like giving this zippy mix as an after-Christmas present instead. I just slip the containers of seasoning, beans and rice into a decorative paper bag. A recipe card completes the package.

- 1 bay leaf
- 1 tablespoon dried sweet pepper flakes
- 1 tablespoon dried minced onion
- 2 teaspoons seasoned salt
- 1 teaspoon ground cumin
- 1 teaspoon sugar
- 1/2 teaspoon celery seed
- 1/2 teaspoon dried minced garlic
- 1/4 teaspoon cayenne pepper
- 1/4 teaspoon crushed red pepper flakes
- 2 cups dry kidney beans
- 1 cup uncooked long grain rice

ADDITIONAL INGREDIENTS:
- 4-1/2 cups water, *divided*
- 1-1/2 to 2 pounds smoked ham hocks
- 1 pound smoked sausage, sliced
- 1/2 teaspoon salt
- Minced fresh parsley, optional

Combine the first 10 ingredients; place in an airtight container. Place beans and rice in separate containers. **Yield:** 1 batch. **To prepare red beans and rice:** Place beans in a Dutch oven or soup kettle; add water to cover by 2 in. Bring to a boil; boil for 2 minutes. Remove from the heat; cover and let stand for 1 hour. Drain. Return beans to pan; add seasoning mix, 2-1/2 cups water and ham hocks. Bring to a boil. Reduce heat; cover and simmer for 1-1/2 hours. Remove ham hocks; cut meat into bite-size pieces and return to pan. Add the sausage. Cover and simmer for 30-40 minutes or until beans are tender and sausage is heated through. Remove bay leaf. Meanwhile, combine rice, salt and remaining water in a saucepan. Bring to a boil. Reduce heat; cover and simmer for 20 minutes or until liquid is absorbed. Remove from the heat; let stand for 5 minutes. Spoon into bowls; top with bean mixture. Garnish with parsley if desired. **Yield:** 4-6 servings.

PRALINE SAUCE
Pat Sturze, Campbell River, British Columbia

A can't-miss treat, this topping can be served at breakfast, lunch or dinner. It's equally delectable drizzled across pancakes, French toast or waffles or served over ice cream.

- 1-1/2 cups dark corn syrup
- 1-1/2 cups light corn syrup
- 1 teaspoon vanilla extract
- 1/8 teaspoon ground cinnamon
- 1/8 teaspoon ground nutmeg
- 1-1/2 cups coarsely chopped pecans, toasted

In a large bowl, combine corn syrups, vanilla, cinnamon and nutmeg until well blended. Stir in pecans. Serve over pancakes, waffles, French toast or ice cream. **Yield:** 4 cups.

● To easily slice a festive fruitcake, cool completely after baking and refrigerate until cold. Cut with a thin sharp non-serrated knife.

Candle Holder Sheds Light Sweetly

EVERY CHRISTMAS, Cheryl Buster takes pains to stir up another colorful batch of Broken Glass Candy in her Fort Collins, Colorado home. "My mom and I made this sparkling red and green candy years ago to give as gifts," she notes. "It's so beautiful packaged in glass jars."

After sampling some sweet pieces in our *CW* test kitchen, we snatched seconds fast! But it was the pretty translucent *look* of Cheryl's candy that got our staff seeing the season in a whole new light. Soon, our creative cooks started experimenting...swirling red and green food coloring into the clear candy for a marbled effect, then molding it into the lovely candle holder you see at left.

Why not try making your own this Christmas? The festive table topper's so quick and easy you won't find yourself burning the candle at both ends to complete it!

(Of course, if you'd prefer to *eat* Cheryl's Broken Glass Candy rather than craft with it, you can do that, too. The recipe's included in the how-to instructions printed below.)

BROKEN GLASS CANDLE HOLDER

3-3/4 cups sugar
1-1/2 cups light corn syrup
   1 cup water
  1/2 teaspoon peppermint *or* cinnamon flavoring
  10 drops *each* green and red food coloring

In a large heavy saucepan, combine sugar, corn syrup and water. Cook, stirring occasionally, over medium-high heat until a candy thermometer reads 300° (hard-crack stage). Remove from the heat; add flavoring. Pour into a well-buttered 15-in. x 10-in. x 1-in. pan. Randomly drop green and red food coloring over candy; swirl a wooden skewer or toothpick through colors to marble (photo 1). Let candy cool until firm, but not completely set, about 20-25 minutes (finger should not leave a dent when pressed into candy, but candy should be warm and bendable). Invert pan and press on pan bottom to release candy in one piece (photo 2). Wrap a sheet of waxed paper around a 2-liter soda bottle; attach with masking tape. Slowly wrap candy around bottle to mold shape, bringing ends together (photo 3). Hold in place until set, about 5 minutes. Remove waxed paper and bottle. Place candy tube on a 10-in. plate. Place a candle in the center. Garnish plate with additional broken glass candy if desired. To store, wrap with plastic wrap and keep in a cool dry place for up to 1 week. **Yield:** 1 candle holder or 2-1/2 pounds of candy. **Editor's Note:** For broken glass candy, prepare recipe as directed. Tint half with green food coloring and half with red. Pour into two buttered 13-in. x 9-in. x 2-in. pans. Cool completely. Remove from pans and break into bite-size pieces.

Tips for Crafting the Candle Holder

• Candle holder can be made 5 to 7 days in advance.
• If you'd like to surround the base of the candle holder with broken glass candy (as is shown in the photo at left), make two batches—one for the candle holder and one to break apart around it.
• Candle may be lit for up to 2 hours before candle holder begins to soften.

1. Using a skewer, swirl food coloring into the candy.

2. Invert a 15-in. x 10-in. pan (a standard jelly roll pan) and gently press on the bottom to release the candy.

3. Slowly mold the pliable candy around a soda bottle that's been wrapped in waxed paper. Finished candle holder will measure 10-1/2 in. high x 5 in. in diameter.

Country Decorating...

Cabin Glows with Holiday Cheer—365 Days a Year!

MAKING MERRY IN MINIATURE is Doris Mottern (below left), who keeps Christmas cabin in Covington, Virginia brimming with festive trims all year—from endeering outdoor decor to gaily decked trees, mantel, more!

FORGET what the calendar says. Within the snug little building behind Doris Mottern's Covington, Virginia home, *every* day is December 25.

"It's where I display all the beautiful Christmas trims I've been collecting since Harold and I were married over 40 years ago," shares this Santa-centered grandmother.

"I dreamed for decades of having a miniature house to hold my treasures. Harold made my wish come true in 1994 when he had the one-room cabin built for me. Nowadays, I never have to put anything away!"

That's even true of the accents decorating the outside. "In the yard," Doris details, "grapevine reindeer always 'play' near the holly bushes we planted. Evergreen boughs outline the porch railing, windows and entry. Above the red door, a festive sign makes plain which season I prefer."

It's the interior, though, that receives the most attention. "The entire space inside the cabin is covered with my knickknacks," says Doris.

"Most visitors flock first to the gas fireplace I've draped with pine boughs, twinkling lights and gold ornaments—mementos of the various states Harold, our three grown children and I have visited over the years."

Another family contribution, curtains crafted from contrasting holly and poinsettia prints, frames the windows. "Daughter Debbie made those without a pattern," Doris notes proudly. "They sure dress up the place."

The same can be said of the adorned trees on opposite ends of the room. Ribbons and glass ornaments trim the larger one, and an angel attired in velvet tops it off. The base, wrapped in plaid fabric, features a charming country village that surrounds it.

A second, slimmer pine is decked in all-American red, white and blue ornaments. "It's my 'Yankee Doodle Dandy', right down to the patriotic Santas standing at the bottom," Doris enthuses.

But that is far from the only spot sporting a Claus or two. Father Christmas figures big in Doris' collection.

For example, an array of jolly old elves, along with other North Pole characters, makes merry in a jelly cupboard she stained green, while still more Kris Kringles clothed in rich hues enliven the top of a small table.

"My favorite fellow takes top billing on the oak floor," Doris points out. "He's an old-fashioned Coca-Cola Santa my husband gave me for our first Christmas. The doll's pulling a wagon Harold made from a soda crate, which I filled with more Coke memorabilia."

Speaking of refreshments, food-related items also embellish a green corner cabinet. "In there, I've paired good-enough-to-eat artificial desserts with dishes I'm particularly fond of," Doris smiles. "It's truly a 'tasteful' holiday display."

For further savoring of the red and green scene, Doris relies on her comfortably rustic sofa. "This is the best seat in the house," she confirms, "especially during our family's annual gift exchange."

Of course, holiday cheer is on hand here at *any* time of year. So Doris' decor can be described indeed as...jolly good!

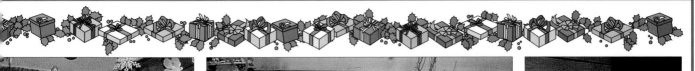

I'll Never Forget...

Newfangled Gift Brightened Our Christmas—for a While!

By Laura Martin-Palmatier of Binghamton, New York

These days, it's difficult to imagine Christmas *not* coming with "batteries included". Seemingly, almost every toy a child receives requires the compact power source to run.

Some 50 years ago, though, household batteries were a wondrous new invention that—as my sisters and I demonstrated one holiday season—still contained more than just a little bit of mystery.

That particular Christmas, when I was 8 years old, my father opened a package and found a most unexpected present…a new flashlight complete with batteries. That was an eye-opener. After all, Mother was still putting us to bed with a kerosene lamp in hand!

Not that night, however. Being thoroughly modern children of the 1940's, Bev and Bea—my sisters—and I realized that flashlight could light the way to more fun for us.

So, when the time arrived, we persuaded Mother to let us put ourselves to bed…and take the flashlight along in place of her usual lamp. Once upstairs, we scurried into our long nighties and crawled under the quilts. Then we made ourselves a tepee in the middle of the bed and spread out with our new comic books and puzzles.

The next night, we did the same. How clever we thought we were! Mother, we were certain, would have no idea how far we were extending our bedtime.

And, perhaps, she wouldn't have—if it weren't for an unforeseen turn Dad's flashlight took. Sometime on the second night, it began to dim. Before long, its glow had become a pale orange.

Suddenly, the shortcomings in our knowledge of Dad's newfangled flashlight became evident. Yes, we understood how it worked—to a degree: Push

> ### "We made ourselves a bed tepee and spread out with comic books and puzzles"

the switch forward and the light would come on. Push the switch back and the light would go off.

But batteries baffled us. For all we knew, they could have a life of 10 years as easily as 10 days. What's more, we'd figured they'd perk up every time we switched the flashlight off.

Next morning, we ourselves woke up well-rested—hoping, in vain, the same could be said of the flashlight's batteries.

It's too bad rechargeable batteries were still decades in the future. That year, they would have made the *perfect* Christmas present for a few girls who hid their light under a quilt instead of a bushel basket! ❦

Grandma's 'Brag' Page

HAPPY HOWLIDAY. With a wagonload of wagging tails, Briley Meeks has a merry litter Christmas, says Grandmother Barbara Garrett of Goodlettsville, Tennessee.

HERE COMES SANTA CLAUZZZ. Though little Jori tried to keep her eyes open, St. Nick caught her napping. Grandma Marjorie Jakusz of Stevens Point, Wisconsin sent snoozer.

CLAUS CALL. Santa couldn't bear to wake baby Jason. "So he told him he'd be back again next Christmas," relates Martha Magoto—grandma of the sugarplum—from Russia, Ohio.

COLD COMFORT. It looks like Joshua Wroblus and the family snowman have a mutual soft spot for one another. Grandma Beverly Mathis, from Riverside, California, shares the far-from-frosty photo of the happy pair.

THREE CHEERS... All wrapped up in festive sweaters fashioned by their grandma, Marilyn Grant, Wallaceburg, Ontario, are cousins Lisa, Alex and Brian. Since they arrived within 4 months, her knitting's now done in triplicate.

Crafter Has the Knack for Fashioning Nicks

NO MATTER if it's December or July, Rhea Breidel's always eager for a Claus encounter of the holiday kind.

"I'm in the spirit all year, crafting Santas from materials I find at rummage sales and auctions," she offers from the home near La Crosse, Wisconsin she and husband Don share.

Tiptoe downstairs to Rhea's basement workshop and you'll find a Santa fantasyland. A satin-clad Father Christmas occupies one corner, while a frontier Santa in fur and snowshoes explores another. A Western Nick decked in denim rides a rocking horse across a bookcase, and a Santa quarterback scores a touchdown beneath a table.

"Occupations and hobbies inspire many of the Santas I hand-fashion for customers," Rhea says, pointing out whiskered lumberjacks, dentists, farmers and fishermen. "My creations range in size from 5-inch ornaments to a 6-1/2-foot figure.

"And just like the real Santa, each of my designs is one of a kind. Since he's a world traveler, I've made Santas that are African, Native American, Russian, Dutch and German.

"As a first step, I mold my faces from papier-mache into unique expres-

CLAUS QUARTERS. "Santas decorate our entire house at Christmas," advises Rhea Breidel (amid Clauses at top left). She crafts Nicks of all shapes and sizes—from elegant gift bearer (at far left) to gnomes (below).

sions," Rhea says as she brushes up a dimpled pink cheek. "The bodies are made of padded wood. Arms and legs are shaped from heavy posable wire.

"My Santa outfits run the gamut from white velvet trimmed in pearls to burlap trousers and jackets made out of patchwork quilts. The beards are formed from exotic wools or mohair to give an authentic appearance.

"Since St. Nick typically has a few tricks in his bag, I add all manner of accents—glasses, antique toys, tiny pine trees, sleds, skates and sleigh bells," she continues. "I trek through our nearby woodland to gather decorative pinecones and twigs I carve into mini walking sticks.

"As one of 12 children, I learned Christmas doesn't come from a store. Of course, Santa Claus was a big part of

HO-HO-HOMADE creations are fashioned from papier-mache, wood, wool, fabric and natural materials, Rhea affirms. Working in craft room (right), she makes sure each holiday "spirit" has his own well-rounded personality.

our holiday celebration. We could barely wait to see if we'd been good enough to merit a visit from him."

Nowadays, Rhea's cleverly crafted Clauses are delivering cheer across the country and clear to Ireland and China. "My Santas are showpieces, not playthings," she clarifies. "Most folks see them as family heirlooms."

There's a festive family feeling behind what Rhea does, too.

"Don constructed my workshop tables, and our grown children are my most valued 'critics'," the country crafter attests. Plus, her grandkids are more than happy to have a grandma who's best friends with Santa Claus!

Editor's Note: *For information on ordering her original Santas, send a self-addressed stamped envelope to Rhea Breidel, N1260 Wuensch Rd., La Crosse WI 54601 or phone her at 1-608/788-4615.*

Teddy Buddy Has a Beary Merry Christmas Sewn Up

EVER SINCE Carolyn Martin started her crafty home business, she's bearly been able to wait for Christmas!

"A teddy is so lovable—it always has a bear hug to spare," the affable grandmother shares about the furry-faced friends she dresses up in her sewing room in East New Market, Maryland. "Each of mine invites my imagination to come play."

Carolyn takes craft bears 8 to 19 inches tall and outfits them in her original designs. Various holidays and seasons inspire her, but her Yuletide teddies are tops in popularity.

"My Christmas bears wear gowns or trousers of red velvet and green gingham and straw hats trimmed with feathers and lace," she says. "They may carry a candy cane or small doll in their paws, or a sprig of mistletoe or holly berries."

There's also a wild side to Carolyn's cuddly-as-can-be cast.

"I trek through nearby woodlands to gather materials—like a wreath of ever-lastings—to use as teddy bear accents," she notes. "I also round up nuts, pine-cones and seed pods.

"Some customers display my bears as collectibles," Carolyn adds. "But the most whimsical are meant just for fun. My children's bear, in washable cottons, has no detachable pieces. Plus, its look says, 'Go ahead and squeeze me!'"

Pressed for time herself, Carolyn barely keeps ahead of requests for her critters. Yet, she sets apart her most heartwarming to contribute to charities and needy children.

"Kids have a great time making up stories and fairy tales to fit the costume their bear is wearing," Carolyn offers. "The same goes for me. When I'm decorating my bears, just about anything seems possible."

It's also obvious age has little bearing on a teddy's appeal, she attests. "A shopper might buy a bear for a grandchild's bedroom—then take another one home for herself."

Of course, *this* grandma doesn't let all her bears get away.

"Here at Christmas," Carolyn chuckles, "I have them napping under the tree and waiting patiently for Santa on the staircase. And more than once, my patient husband, Tom, has gone to sit in a chair…and discovered that a bear is already perched there!"

Editor's Note: *For a flyer and price list on her whimsical bears, write to Carolyn Martin, P.O. Box 279, East New Market MD 21631. And if you'd like to try a craft project that bears out how cute her creations are, just glance over at the next page!* 🌿

DEN OF DELIGHTS is what a room becomes when it's softened by cute Yule bruins crafted by Carolyn Martin (topping one off above).

Craft Section...

Dress Up Your Own Festive Teddy Bear

CARE to clothe a bear as fashionably as Carolyn Martin does (see article on previous page)? No problem!

Here, Carolyn eagerly explains how to make merry togs for a 12-inch-tall teddy bear. Pair her instructions with a handful of simple supplies, and you'll quickly have a crafty critter to brighten your home for the holidays.

Materials Needed:

12-inch craft bear
6-inch x 42-inch piece of Christmas print for skirt
Pre-gathered or ruffled lace—1 yard of 2-inch-wide white and 1-3/4 yards of 1-1/2-inch-wide red
Ribbon—1 yard of 1/2-inch-wide red satin, 1-1/2 yards of 5/8-inch-wide red grosgrain and 1/2 yard of 1/4-inch-wide red satin
1/2 yard of 1/4-inch-wide elastic
Sinamay or straw hat to fit
Assorted decorative trims*
Glue gun and glue sticks
Scissors
Matching thread
Standard sewing supplies

*Carolyn used ribbon and silk roses, flat-backed acrylic hearts, nylon netting and iridescent string pearls to decorate her bear.

Finished Size: Seated bear is approximately 10 inches tall, including hat.

Directions:
SKIRT: Sew short ends of skirt fabric right sides together with a 1/2-in. seam. Press seam open.

Press under a 1/4-in. hem along one long edge. Pin right side of red lace to edge of hem on wrong side of fabric, allowing nearly all of the lace to extend beyond hem. Straight-stitch lace in place.

Along remaining long edge, fold 1/4 in. to wrong side. Fold down 3/8 in. again to wrong side to form a channel for the elastic and press. Using matching thread and straight stitch, stitch close to first fold, leaving an opening. Attach safety pin to elastic and insert through opening into channel. Adjust elastic to fit bear's waist. Stitch ends of elastic to secure and stitch opening closed.

Put skirt on bear with seam in back.
LACE TOP: Cut one piece of red lace and one piece of white lace, each 11 in. long. Layer the red lace on top of the

white lace with gathered edges matching and stitch together along this edge. Fold and glue ends back about 1 in.

With red lace on top, position one end at center front of skirt waist and glue into place. Drape lace over top of shoulder as shown in photo above and glue lace close to neck edge. Glue opposite end of lace to center back of skirt waist, adjusting length if necessary.

Repeat for other side of lace top.

HAT: Cut a piece of white lace to fit around brim of hat where it meets the crown and glue lace into place.

Decorate the rest of the hat as desired.
FINISHING: Cut grosgrain ribbon into three 18-in. pieces. Tie a bow around each wrist. Tie remaining piece in a bow and glue it to back of skirt at waist.

Tie 1/2-in.-wide satin ribbon in a bow around bear's neck.

Cut 1/4-in.-wide satin ribbon into three 6-in. pieces and tie each in a bow. Glue bows randomly to hem of skirt.

Referring to the photo above for inspiration, add your choice of additional decorative ribbons and trims to embellish your bear. ❦

Bright Box Harbors Yuletide Sweetness

FILLED to the brim with country flavor, this container will attract as much attention as the candy inside it!

It's a treat to make, too, according to Teri Bloom of Uniontown, Pennsylvania. "The plastic canvas I used is easy to handle," she notes. "And the long stitches make the project extra speedy."

Materials Needed:

Charts on next page
10-1/2-inch x 13-1/2-inch sheets of 7-count plastic canvas—one each of clear for stitching and red for lining
Worsted-weight yarn—40 yards of green and 15 yards of red
Purchased green gift bow
White tacky glue
Size 16 tapestry needle
Scissors

Finished Size: Gift box is about 4 inches square x 4 inches high without bow.

Directions:

Being sure to count the bars and not the holes, cut plastic canvas according to the charts on next page. Also cut one red plastic canvas piece 26 bars x 26 bars and one clear plastic canvas piece 26 bars x 26 bars for bottom.

Cut 20-in. to 24-in. lengths of yarn. Do not knot the yarn on back of work. Instead, leave a 1-in. tail on the back and catch it in the first few stitches. To end a yarn, run yarn on back of canvas under completed stitches of the same color and clip close to work.

Stitch each panel on clear canvas following charts for stitches and colors of yarn used, leaving outside edges unstitched. In addition, stitch clear plastic bottom using green and Continental stitch, leaving outside edges unstitched. See Fig. 1 for stitch illustrations.

ASSEMBLY: Place one red canvas side panel on the back of a matching stitched gift box side panel. The red canvas will line the gift box and hide the stitching. Using matching colors, whipstitch the top edges together. Repeat for the remaining three side panels.

Referring to photo above right and Fig. 2, assemble gift box as follows: Using green, whipstitch side edges of each gift box side panel together, keeping red canvas to the inside.

Whipstitch the stitched bottom and matching red canvas of the gift box to the bottom edges of the sides, using matching yarns as before and keeping red canvas to the inside.

Place red canvas behind matching stitched panels of lid as for gift box. Assemble the lid in the same way as gift box, whipstitching top of lid to top edges of the lid side panels.

Place completed lid on gift box and glue bow to center top of lid.

Fig. 1

Slanted Gobelin stitch

Whipstitch

Continental stitch

Fig. 2

Assembly Diagram
With matching red canvas panels on back of stitched panels, whipstitch together as instructed.

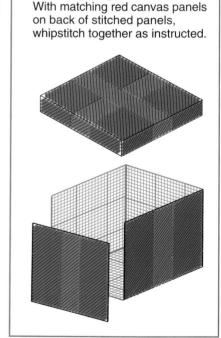

PLASTIC CANVAS GIFT BOX CHARTS

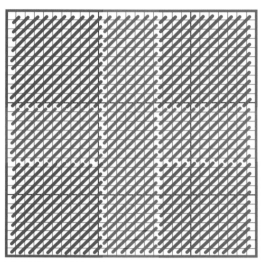

LID TOP PANEL CHART
28 x 28 bars
Cut 1—red plastic canvas
Cut and stitch 1—clear plastic canvas

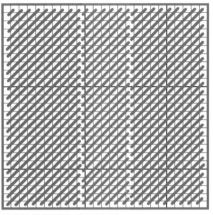

SIDE PANEL CHART
26 x 26 bars
Cut 4—red plastic canvas
Cut and stitch 4—clear plastic canvas

COLOR KEY
SLANTED GOBELIN
/ Red
/ Green
WHIPSTITCH
− Red
− Green

LID SIDE PANEL CHART
28 x 6 bars
Cut 4—red plastic canvas
Cut and stitch 4—clear plastic canvas

Easy-to-Plait Trimmers Add Twist to Presents

TIE DOWN your package wrapping this December with a host of happy wreaths you can braid from festive fabric strips.

In addition to topping presents, the wreaths can serve as nifty napkin rings or tree-branch brighteners, relates designer Chris Pfefferkorn, New Braunfels, Texas. "My project's a fun one for youngsters to try, too," she adds.

Materials Needed (for one wreath):
Bias strips of three coordinating Christmas print fabrics—each 1-1/2 inches x 10 inches
12 inches of 1/4-inch-wide green satin ribbon
Small safety pin or tube turner
Standard sewing supplies

Finished Size: Each braided wreath

measures about 3 inches across without bow.

Directions:
Fold a bias strip with right sides together and stitch 3/8 in. from fold, making a 10-in.-long tube. Do not trim seam.

Turn tube right side out by attaching the safety pin to one end and pulling it through the tube or by using tube turner. Do not press. Repeat two more times, making a total of three tubes.

Whipstitch one end of each tube together and make an 8-in.-long flat braid. See Fig. 1.

Shape the braid into a circle about 3 in. across and stitch the ends together to form wreath. Trim ends as needed.

Wrap ribbon around wreath where strips are joined to hide stitches. Tie ribbon into a small bow as shown in photo and trim ends at an angle.

Fig. 1 Making flat braid

Jolly Jingling Quilt Rings in Season

START the holidays off on the right note by stitching up this harmonious Christmas quilt.

Michele Crawford, from Spokane, Washington, combined applique and patchwork to create her well-toned wall hanging or table topper—one that keeps your Christmas budget in mind. She reports you can make use of your on-hand holiday fabric scraps to make it.

Materials Needed:
Patterns on next page
Tracing paper
Template plastic
1/2 yard of paper-backed fusible web
44-inch-wide 100% cotton fabrics—
   1-1/3 yards of red solid for backing and hanging sleeve, 1-1/2 yards of white for squares and piecing, 1/4 yard of green Christmas print for bells, 1/3 yard of red metallic print for inside border, 1/2 yard of large Christmas print for outside border and 1/3 yard each of red and green prints or scraps of red and green prints for piecing (Michele used an assortment of prints, stripes, plaids and Christmas prints to create a scrappy look.)
5 yards of red extra-wide double-fold bias tape for binding*
Nine 12mm gold jingle bells
Matching all-purpose thread*
Red quilting thread*
Gold metallic thread*
Transparent nylon monofilament thread*
Package of red baby rickrack
1-1/2 yards of 1/2-inch-wide red ribbon
45-inch square of lightweight quilt batting
Rotary cutter and mat (optional)
Quilter's marking pen or pencil
Safety pins (optional)
Quilting and hand-sewing needles
Standard sewing supplies
42 inches of 1/2-inch dowel or lattice strip for hanging
* Michele used the following Coats & Clark products: Dual Duty Plus Thread, Transparent Nylon Monofilament Thread, Gold Metallic Thread, Extra Strong Hand Quilting Thread and Bias Tape.

Finished Size: Wall hanging measures 43-1/2 inches square.

Directions:
Machine-wash, dry and press all fabrics if desired.

Do all piecing with accurate 1/4-in. seams and right sides of fabric together. Press seams toward darker fabrics when possible, unless otherwise directed.

CUTTING: Accurately cut fabrics using rotary cutter and quilter's ruler or mark fabrics using ruler and quilt marker and cut with scissors. Cut all of the strips crosswise from selvage to selvage.

From white, cut three 3-1/2-in.-wide strips and nine 2-3/8-in.-wide strips. Cut these strips into thirty-six 3-1/2-in. squares and one hundred forty-four 2-3/8-in. squares. Also cut the 2-3/8-in. squares in half diagonally, forming 288 triangles. From remaining white, cut nine 6-1/2-in. squares.

From red print or a variety of red prints, cut thirty-six 3-in. squares. Cut each of these squares in half diagonally to form 72 triangles.

From green print or a variety of green prints, cut thirty-six 3-in. squares. Cut each of these squares in half diagonally to form 72 triangles.

From red metallic print, cut four 1-1/2-in.-wide strips for inside border and four 3-in. squares for corners.

From large Christmas print, cut four 3-in.-wide strips for outside border.

From red solid, cut a 44-in. square for backing and a 3-in. x 44-in. strip for hanging sleeve.

APPLIQUEING: Trace the bell pattern onto the paper side of the fusible web nine times, leaving a 1/2-in. space around each shape. Fuse onto wrong side of green Christmas print, following the manufacturer's directions. Cut out shapes along traced lines.

Fuse one bell shape to the center of each 6-1/2-in. white square.

PIECING: Pieced Strips (make 36): Referring to Fig. 1, sew the diagonal edge of a white triangle to a short edge of a print triangle. Repeat on remaining short edge of print triangle, making a total of 144 rectangles.

Stitch the long edges of the rectangles together in groups of four, alternating red and green prints in each group and making sure all triangles point in the same direction. See Fig. 2. Make a total of 36 pieced strips.

Stitch a 3-1/2-in. white square to the top and bottom of 18 of the pieced strips as shown in Fig. 3.

ASSEMBLY: Referring to photo at the

left, lay out all pieces, placing pieced strips as shown.

Sew a pieced strip without the white corner blocks to the top and bottom edges of each center block, carefully matching corners. Then sew strips with white corner blocks to each side. Repeat, making a total of nine quilt blocks.

Sew blocks together as shown in photo, forming three rows. Sew rows together.

Borders: Center and sew one red metallic border strip to one side edge of wall hanging and trim length to fit. Stitch another border strip to opposite side and trim length to fit. Add top and bottom border strips in the same manner.

Cut a large Christmas print border strip to fit top edge of wall hanging and sew a red metallic square to each end of strip. Repeat for bottom border. Set aside.

Sew large Christmas print border strips to each side of wall hanging and trim length to fit.

Stitch border strips with corner blocks to top and bottom edges, carefully matching corners.

QUILTING: Place backing wrong side up on a flat surface and smooth out wrinkles. Place batting over backing and smooth out. Center wall hanging top over batting, right side up, and smooth out. Use safety pins to pin layers together or hand-baste through all the three layers, stitching or pinning from center to corners, then every 4 in. across horizontally and vertically.

Using monofilament thread on top and red thread on the bobbin, stitch-in-the-ditch along border seams, around the center squares and remaining edges of corner squares.

Using red thread, straight-stitch rickrack to each bell where shown on pattern.

Blanket-stitch around each bell using gold thread. See Fig. 4.

Trace heart onto template plastic. Cut out. Using quilt marker, trace around heart in center of each white square. Hand-stitch over traced lines using red quilting thread and running stitch. See Fig. 5.

BINDING: Press 1/2 in. of one short edge of double-fold bias tape to wrong side. Stitch binding to front of wall hanging, matching raw edges and mitering corners. Trim off excess, leaving a 1-in. overlap. Fold binding to back and hand-stitch folded edge over seam to backing fabric. Remove basting thread/pins.

FINISHING: Cut ribbon into nine 6-in. pieces and tie each in a bow. Hand-stitch a bow to the top of each bell and trim ends at an angle.

Hand-stitch a jingle bell to the bottom of each bell applique.

Press 1/2 in. to wrong side along each long edge of hanging sleeve. Turn under 1/4 in. at each short end of sleeve. Turn under 1/4 in. again and stitch. Center sleeve along back of wall hanging just below the top binding and hand-stitch long edges along each fold to backing fabric, forming hanging sleeve. Insert dowel or lattice strip.

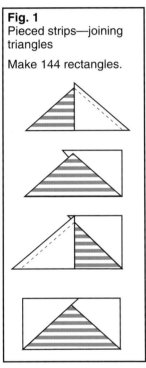

Fig. 1
Pieced strips—joining triangles

Make 144 rectangles.

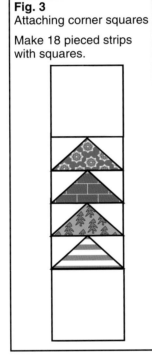

Fig. 3
Attaching corner squares

Make 18 pieced strips with squares.

Fig. 4
Blanket stitch

Fig. 5
Running stitch

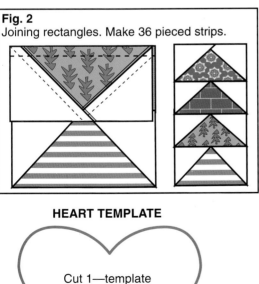

Fig. 2
Joining rectangles. Make 36 pieced strips.

HEART TEMPLATE

Cut 1—template plastic

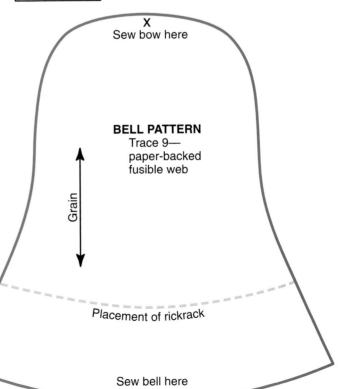

X
Sew bow here

BELL PATTERN
Trace 9—
paper-backed
fusible web

Grain

Placement of rickrack

Sew bell here
X

Fine-line black permanent marker
Scissors

Finished Size: Christmas tree is 4-3/4 inches tall x 3-1/2 inches across. Stocking is 3-1/4 inches tall x 3-1/4 inches across.

Directions:
Trace patterns on this page onto tracing paper and cut out. Trace around each pattern onto aluminum. Cut out shapes using tin snips or utility scissors.

Tape pattern onto appropriate shape and place on protective surface. Punch design using nail and hammer, moving from dot to dot. Remove pattern and turn shape over. The smooth side will be the back.

PAINTING: Referring to photo at left and patterns for color placement, apply paint to each ornament just inside punched lines. When dry, use marker to add lines to heel and toe of stocking.

FINISHING: Glue a clothespin to the back of each ornament, placing the open end of clothespin at bottom of the design so trim will sit on the top of the tree branch.

Punch Up Today's Decor —With Metal Tree Trims

LIKE to put a nostalgic stamp on your Yuletide tree? Try these pretty-as-can-be ornaments that feature old-fashioned tin-punching.

Sandra Smith, who hails from Florissant, Missouri, shares the pair of holiday trims. She notes that anyone can tackle the technique in a flash. So start punching away on these bright beauties without delay today!

Materials Needed (for both trims):
Patterns on this page
Tracing paper and pencil

8-inch x 8-inch sheet of aluminum flashing (available at most hardware stores)
Finishing nails and hammer
Hard protective surface (such as pressed wood board)
Tin snips or utility scissors
Enamel paint—green, red, white and yellow
Small flat paintbrush
Paper plate or palette
Glue gun and glue sticks
Two 3-1/4-inch wooden spring clothespins
Masking tape

Note: The patterns are given in reverse so they will face in the correct direction when completed.

STOCKING
Trace 1—tracing paper
Cut 1—aluminum

CHRISTMAS TREE
Trace 1—tracing paper
Cut 1—aluminum

Snow Doily Delivers a White Christmas

WHEREVER you live, you can create a winter wonderland—by including this snowflake decoration among your bright holiday trims.

The lacy crocheted doily developed by Emma Willey of Winston, Oregon will have you hooked from the moment you start crocheting. So get set to stitch up one for yourself—followed by several others for those folks on your Christmas list.

Materials Needed:
One 400-yard ball of white size 10 crochet cotton
Size 6 (1.75mm) steel crochet hook
Tapestry needle and scissors

Finished Size: Doily measures about 13 inches square.

Gauge: 8 dc = 1 inch.

Special Stitches:
2 dc Cluster (2 dc Cl): Holding back last lp of each dc, dc in each of next two ch-3 sps, yo, draw through all lps on hk.

Directions:
FIRST MOTIF: Ch 6; join with sl st in beginning ch to form a ring.

Round 1: Ch 3 (counts as first dc here and throughout), dc in ring 15 times; join with sl st in top of beginning ch-3: 16 dc.

Round 2: Ch 3, dc in same sp, ch 3; * skip 1 dc, work 2 dc in next dc, ch 3; rep from * around, join with sl st in top of beginning ch-3.

Round 3: Ch 3, dc in same sp, work 2 dc in next dc, ch 3; * work 2 dc in each of next 2 dc, ch 3; rep from * around, join with sl st in top of beginning ch-3.

Round 4: Ch 3, dc in same sp, dc in each of next 2 dc, work 2 dc in next dc, ch 3; * work 2 dc in first dc, 1 dc in each of next 2 dc, 2 dc in next dc, ch 3; rep from * around, join with sl st in top of beginning ch-3.

Round 5: * Ch 7, skip 4 dc, sc in next dc, work 3 sc in next ch-3 sp, sc in next dc; rep from * around, working the last sc in the base of beginning ch-7.

Round 6: Sl st into ch-7 sp, ch 3, work (3 dc, ch 3, 4 dc) in same sp, ch 1, sc in center sc, ch 1; * work (4 dc, ch 3, 4 dc) in next ch-7 sp, ch 1, sc in center sc, ch 1; rep from * around, join with sl st in top of beginning ch-3. Fasten off. One motif completed.

SECOND MOTIF: Following directions for first motif, work Rounds 1-5. Making six of the eight points of Round 6, join the first and second motifs with wrong sides together at the next two points as follows: * In next ch-7 sp, work 4 dc, ch 1, making next point of new motif, sc in any ch-3 sp (point) of motif to be joined, ch 1, work 4 dc in same ch-7 sp of new motif, ch 1, sc in center sc, ch 1; rep from * one more time, join with sl st in top of beginning ch-3. Fasten off.

THIRD MOTIF: Work as for second motif and join it to side of second motif, making a horizontal row consisting of three motifs.

FOURTH MOTIF: Work as for second motif and join it to bottom of first motif, starting second horizontal row.

FIFTH MOTIF: Following directions for first motif, work Rounds 1-5. Making four of the eight points of Round 6, join the fifth motif to side of fourth motif and to bottom of second motif as follows: * In next ch-7 sp, work 4 dc, ch 1, making next point of new motif, sc in ch-3 sp (point) of motif to be joined, ch 1, work 4 dc in same ch-7 sp of new motif, ch 1, sc in center sc, ch 1; rep from * three more times, join with sl st in top of beginning ch-3. Fasten off.

SIXTH MOTIF: Work as for fifth motif and join to side of fifth motif and bottom of third motif.

SEVENTH MOTIF: Work as for second motif and join to bottom of fourth motif, starting third horizontal row.

EIGHTH MOTIF: Work as for fifth motif and join to side of seventh motif and bottom of fifth motif.

NINTH MOTIF: Work as for fifth motif and join to side of eighth motif and bottom of sixth motif.

FILL-IN MOTIFS: Ch 6; join with sl st in beginning ch to form a ring.

Round 1: Ch 3, dc in ring 15 times; join with sl st in top of beginning ch-3: 16 dc.

Round 2: Ch 4, with wrong sides together, sc in ch-sp of a joined point of motif, ch 4, skip 1 dc, sc in next dc of ring; * ch 4, sc in next ch-sp of a joined point of motif, ch 4, skip 1 dc, sc in next dc of ring; rep from * around (eight points fastened); join with sl st in first st of round. Fasten off.

Rep three more times, joining points of remaining motifs to fill-in motifs.

EDGING: Round 1: Join with a sl st in any outside point, * ch 7, sc in next

sc between points, ch 7, sc in next point or in sc that joins two points; rep from * around, ending with ch 7.

Round 2: Sl st to third ch of next ch-7 sp, ch 3, work (1 dc, ch 3, 2 dc) shell in same ch-7 sp, ch 3; * work (2 dc, ch 3, 2 dc) shell in next ch-7 sp, ch 3; rep from * around, join with sl st in top of beginning ch-3.

Round 3: Sl st to ch-3 sp of shell, ch 3, work (1 dc, ch 3, 2 dc) shell in same sp, ch 3, sc in next ch-3 sp, ch 3; * work (2 dc, ch 3, 2 dc) shell in next shell, ch 3, sc in next ch-3 sp, ch 3; rep from * around, join with sl st in top of beginning ch 3.

Round 4: Sl st to center of shell, ch 3 for first dc, ch 3, sl st in third ch from hk to form a picot; * ch 3, work 2 dc Cl over next 2 ch-3 sps, ch 3, dc in ch-3 sp of next shell, ch-3 picot in dc; rep from * around, ending last rep with ch 3, work 2 dc Cl over last 2 ch-3 sps, ch 3, sl st in first ch of round. Fasten off.

Weave in all loose ends.

ABBREVIATIONS	
ch(s)	chain(s)
Cl	cluster
dc(s)	double crochet(s)
hk	hook
lp(s)	loop(s)
rep	repeat
sc	single crochet
sl st	slip stitch
sp(s)	space(s)
st(s)	stitches(s)
yo	yarn over
*	Instructions following asterisk are repeated as directed

Pretty Holiday Picture's Painted by Her Jolly Jar

YOU'LL be hard-pressed to keep the lid on this craft!

For starters, the snowy vista you paint on is a real scene-stealer. What's more, attests crafter Linda Lover of Byron, Michigan, the design's a breeze to add to almost any plain glass jar.

Once the paint is dry, you can fill yours with candies, or add buttons or potpourri. "You can also paint several in different sizes to create a canister set," Linda advises.

Materials Needed:
Pattern on this page
Tracing paper and pencil
Typing paper
Jar with screw-on lid
Paper plate or palette
*Acrylic craft paints—black, blue, brown, green, red, white and yellow**

Paintbrushes—Nos. 6 and 2 flat and No. 1 liner
Transparent or masking tape
Linda used Delta Ceramcoat Perm-enamel paints.

Finished Size: Candy jar is 6 inches high x 3 inches across. Design area is 4 inches tall x 5 inches wide and can be enlarged or reduced on a copy machine to fit other size jars.

Directions:
Trace pattern below onto tracing paper with a pencil. Tape the traced pattern over a piece of typing paper and trim both papers to fit inside the jar.

Roll pattern loosely and slip it into jar so traced design is visible from the outside of the jar. Tape pattern to inside of jar as needed to keep it in place.

PAINTING: Place small dabs of paint on paper plate or palette as needed. Paint as directed below, applying one coat for a translucent look. Or apply a second coat for complete coverage, allowing drying time between coats.

Using No. 6 flat brush, paint jar lid blue, tree green and snowman's head and body white. Let dry.

Using No. 2 flat brush, paint hat black, scarf yellow and tree trunk brown. Let dry.

Using liner, paint hatband and heart red, zigzags on scarf green and star on hat yellow.

Mix a bit of yellow and red paint together to make orange and, using liner, paint snowman's nose. When dry, add red detail lines.

Use handle of brush to dab on black paint for snowman's eyes and buttons.

Using flat brush and white, lightly paint snow on and under tree and under snowman. Use handle of brush to dab on random dots of white paint around design for snowflakes.

Using liner and white, paint snowflakes on top of lid as shown in photo above. Let dry. Fill jar with candy.

CANDY JAR PATTERN
Trace 1—tracing paper
Paint as directed

Stitched Trim Brims With Yule's Cheer

WITH holiday images galore, this colorful stitchery will bring the season's sights well into focus at your house. Renee Dent of Conrad, Montana picked her favorite festive motifs, along with a handful of holiday hues, to patch together her idea.

Materials Needed:

Chart on this page
5-inch square of white 14-count Aida cloth
DMC six-strand embroidery floss in colors listed on color key
Two 3-1/4-inch squares of lightweight cardboard
3-1/4-inch square of lightweight batting for padding
5-inch square of Christmas print for backing
14 inches of 1/2-inch-wide pre-gathered white lace
6 inches of 1/4-inch-wide white satin ribbon
Size 24 tapestry needle
Scissors
White tacky glue

Finished Size: Trim is 3-3/4 inches square. Design area is 46 stitches wide x 46 stitches high.

Directions:

Zigzag or overcast edges of Aida cloth to prevent fraying. Fold cloth in half lengthwise, then fold in half crosswise to determine center and mark this point. To find center of chart, draw lines across chart connecting arrows. Begin stitching at this point so design will be centered.

Working with 18-inch lengths of six-strand floss, separate strands and use three strands for cross-stitching and one strand for backstitching and French knots. See Fig. 1 for stitch illustrations.

Each square on chart equals one stitch worked over a set of fabric threads. Use colors indicated on color key to complete cross-stitching, then backstitching and French knots.

Do not knot floss on back of work. Instead, leave a short tail of floss on back of work and hold it in place while working the first few stitches around it. To end a strand, run needle under a few neighboring stitches in back before cutting floss close to work.

When stitching is completed, wash gently in lukewarm water if necessary. Press wrong side up on terry towel to dry.

FINISHING: Glue batting to one piece of cardboard with edges matching. With right side up, center completed cross-stitch design over padded side of cardboard. Glue edges of Aida cloth to back of cardboard piece, carefully smoothing front and mitering corners.

In same way, cover other cardboard with backing fabric, omitting batting.

Glue straight edge of lace to back of padded cross-stitch piece so lace extends beyond edge of piece, overlapping edges of lace along the top edge. Fold ribbon in half and glue ends to top center back of stitched piece to form a hanging loop.

With wrong sides together and edges matching, glue stitched design to covered back.

CROSS-STITCHED TRIM CHART

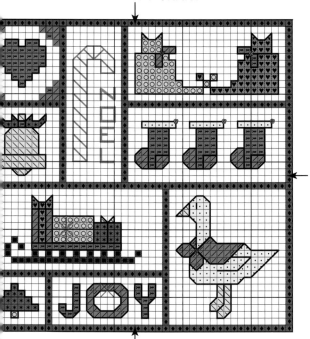

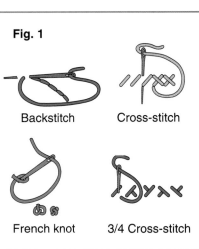

Fig. 1

Backstitch	Cross-stitch
French knot	3/4 Cross-stitch

CROSS-STITCHED TRIM COLOR KEY

		DMC
■	Black	310
◆	Light Navy Blue	312
⋈	Dark Coral	349
◎	Light Gold	676
✳	Dark Christmas Green	700
▨	Kelly Green	702
◹	Medium Topaz	725
♥	Very Light Pearl Gray	762
⊡	Ultra Pale Yellow	3823

BACKSTITCHING
— Dark Coral—
   candy cane, package
   bow, wreath bow 349
— Kelly Green—
   "Noel" 702
— Black-Brown 3371

FRENCH KNOTS
❀ Dark Coral—
   center of green bows
   on cat and goose 349
❀ Kelly Green—
   center of red bow on cat,
   hangers on stockings 702

Appliqued Mat's an Ornate Bloomer

A GREEN THUMB'S not necessary to grow perfect poinsettias. Just make this place mat shared by Winnie Malone of Westerville, Ohio. You'll have pleasing bouquets to top your table for many Christmases to come.

In addition to individual mats, you can use the design as part of a centerpiece. Plus, it makes a stunning gift or a craft bazaar best-seller.

Materials Needed (for one):
Patterns on next page
Tracing paper and pencil
44-inch-wide 100% cotton or cotton-blend fabrics—1/2 yard of white solid, 1/2 yard of red solid for backing and appliques, scrap of green solid for appliques and 1 yard of red pin-dot for binding
1/2 yard of fleece or lightweight batting
1/4 yard of paper-backed fusible web
1/2 yard of tear-away stabilizer or typing paper
All-purpose sewing thread—green and red
Quilting thread—green and red
Six-strand embroidery floss—green and yellow
Embroidery needle
Water-soluble quilt marker
Black medium-point permanent marker
Paper grocery sack
Standard sewing supplies

Finished Size: Place mat measures 12 inches x 17-1/2 inches.

Directions:
Trace patterns on next page onto paper side of fusible web, leaving about 1 in. between shapes. Cut apart shapes and fuse to wrong side of the fabrics as directed on patterns. Transfer inside stitching lines by straight-stitching along these lines through the paper backing. Cut out the leaves and flowers on the outside traced lines.

From grocery sack, cut a 12-in. x 17-1/2-in. rectangle. Fold rectangle in half lengthwise, and then in half crosswise, forming a 6-in. x 8-3/4-in. rectangle. Referring to Fig. 1, measure 7-3/8 in. diagonally from center folds and mark position. Draw an arc connecting this mark to the straight edges of the rectangle. Cut through all layers and unfold for place mat pattern.

Place pattern on right side of white fabric, matching folds to grain of fabric. Trace around pattern with water-soluble marker. Cut out fabric 1 in. outside traced line. In the same way, cut one each from red solid fabric and batting.

APPLIQUEING: Remove paper backing from appliques. Arrange appliques on right side of white fabric as shown in photo above. Fuse in place following manufacturer's directions

Pin stabilizer to wrong side of fabric behind the appliques. Machine-stitch around shapes with a narrow satin stitch, using green thread to stitch around leaves and red thread to stitch around flowers and over inside stitching lines. Bring threads to wrong side and secure.

MARKING AND EMBROIDERY: Referring to photo for placement, trace a 5-1/2-in. x 3-in. oval centered on right side of white fabric with water-soluble marker. Using water-soluble marker, write "Merry Christmas" inside oval. Stem-stitch over lettering with one strand of green embroidery floss. See Fig. 2 on next page.

For quilting pattern, trace applique patterns onto tracing paper, using black medium-point marker and omitting under-lap lines. Cut apart.

Flip quilting patterns over and place under white fabric, arranging them as shown in photo. Trace over patterns using water-soluble marker.

Using two strands of yellow embroidery floss, stitch French knots in center of traced and appliqued poinsettias. See Fig. 2.

QUILTING: Place the backing wrong side up on a flat surface and smooth out wrinkles. Place batting over backing and smooth out. Center place mat top over batting, right side up, and smooth out. Hand-baste all three layers together, stitching from center to edges, then every 4 in. across horizontally and vertically.

Using red quilting thread and running stitch, hand-stitch through all layers 1/8 in. from outside edges of appliques and on traced quilting lines of flowers and leaves. See Fig. 2.

In the same way, hand-stitch around center oval using green quilting thread.

Trim all layers even, cutting along place mat outline on white fabric

BINDING: From red pin-dot, make a bias strip 2-1/2 in. wide x 54 in. long. Fold strip in half lengthwise, wrong sides together, and press. With raw edges of strip matching raw edges of place mat, fold back beginning of strip 1/2 in., then stitch binding to place mat, overlapping the ends. Trim excess. Fold binding to back of place mat, covering stitching. Hand-stitch to backing.

Fig. 1
Cutting place mat pattern

Fold

Fold

7-3/8 in.

Draw arc and cut along line

Discard

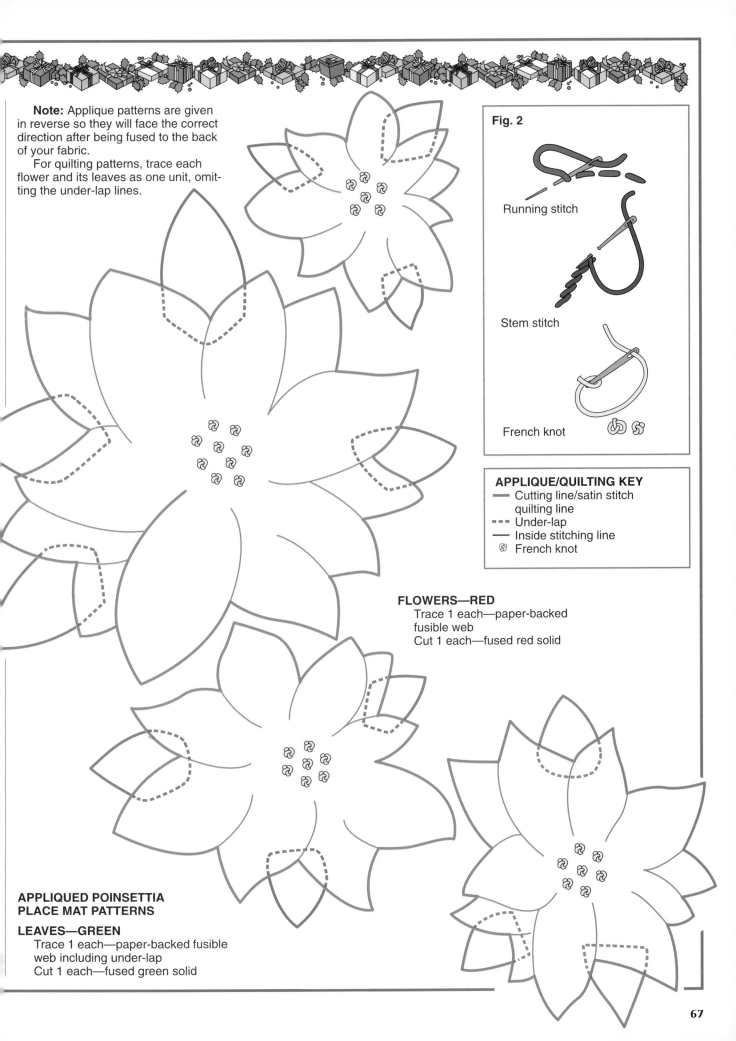

Note: Applique patterns are given in reverse so they will face the correct direction after being fused to the back of your fabric.

For quilting patterns, trace each flower and its leaves as one unit, omitting the under-lap lines.

Fig. 2

Running stitch

Stem stitch

French knot

APPLIQUE/QUILTING KEY
— Cutting line/satin stitch quilting line
--- Under-lap
— Inside stitching line
⑨ French knot

FLOWERS—RED
Trace 1 each—paper-backed fusible web
Cut 1 each—fused red solid

APPLIQUED POINSETTIA PLACE MAT PATTERNS

LEAVES—GREEN
Trace 1 each—paper-backed fusible web including under-lap
Cut 1 each—fused green solid

Scrappy Centerpiece Salutes Season

BY MARCHING OUT this army of cheerful soldiers to parade brightly on the dinner table, you'll marshal a spirited—and "centsible"—start to your family's festivities.

Shirley Wiskow shares the plastic canvas topper. She made it for her Jackson, New Jersey home from scraps of yarn and snippets of silk holly…the kinds of materials you can easily drum up from among your on-hand craft supplies.

Materials Needed:
Chart on next page
One 12-inch x 18-inch sheet of 7-count plastic canvas
Worsted-weight yarn—scraps or one skein each of red, flesh, white metallic, black and blue
6 yards of gold metallic braid
Purchased 9-inch x 1-1/2-inch Styrofoam disc or 9-inch circle cut from Styrofoam
9-inch circle of cardboard
10-inch circle of white felt
Plastic canvas needle
3-inch x 6-inch white candle
Artificial holly—about 35 sprigs with picks
Tacky white glue
Black permanent marker
Craft knife and scissors

Finished Size: Centerpiece is about 9 inches across x 6 inches high, including the candle.

Directions:
Using black marker and following chart at right, draw outline of seven soldiers along one long edge of plastic canvas. Be sure to follow chart for exact numbers of holes and bars and to leave six holes between the jackets of the soldiers. Repeat along opposite long edge.

Being sure to leave the bars along the outline, cut out the two strips of seven soldiers for a total of 14 soldiers.

Cut 18-in. lengths of yarn. Do not knot the yarn on back of work. Instead, leave a 1-in. tail on the back and catch it in the first few stitches. To end a strand, run yarn on back of canvas under completed stitches of the same color and clip close to work.

Following the chart and referring to Fig. 1 for stitch illustrations, stitch each soldier as directed. Then stitch each space between the soldiers, leaving bottom edge unstitched.

When stitching is complete, use white metallic to whipstitch the ends together, following the stitch pattern to form a ring. Then use white metallic to overcast bottom edge of the ring.

FINISHING: Check the size of the foam disc with the size of the completed ring. If the Styrofoam disc is too large to fit inside the completed ring, stand the disc on end and roll the disc on a hard surface to compress the outside edge. Or use a craft knife to trim the disc to fit inside the completed ring.

Place the candle on center top of disc and trace around the base of the candle. Using craft knife, cut just inside the traced line and remove and discard the center circle.

Center cardboard circle on top of felt circle. Wrap and glue felt to cover cardboard, smoothing and clipping edges of felt as needed. Place covered circle, felt side down, on flat surface. Center and glue foam disc over covered circle.

Slip completed ring over disc. Glue Styrofoam scraps between ring and disc if needed. Spot-glue ring to disc. Place candle in opening. Insert holly sprigs into disc around candle as in photo above left.

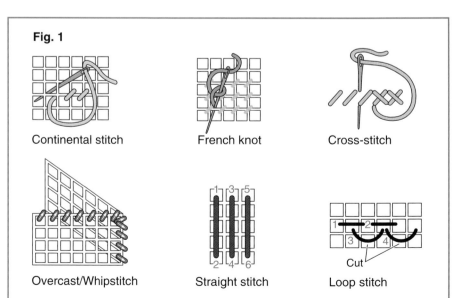

Fig. 1

Continental stitch

French knot

Cross-stitch

Overcast/Whipstitch

Straight stitch

Loop stitch

Cut

SOLDIER CENTERPIECE
COLOR KEY
✎ Red
✎ Flesh
✎ White Metallic (2 strands)
STRAIGHT STITCH
▮ Black (2 strands)
▬ Red (1 ply)
LOOP STITCH
✎ Black
FRENCH KNOT
◉ Blue
CROSS-STITCH
✕ Gold Metallic Braid
OVERCAST/WHIPSTITCH
▬ Red
= Flesh
▬ Black
= White Metallic (2 strands)

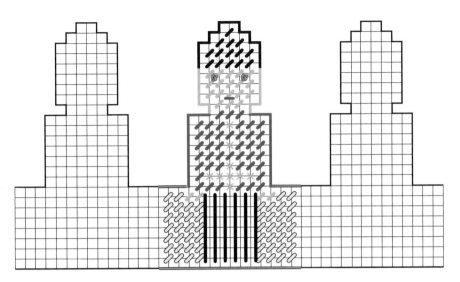

SOLDIER CENTERPIECE CHART
Completed chart equals 25 bars x 198 bars.
Trace around chart and duplicate pattern as directed.
Cut 2 strips of 7 soldiers each.

Tasty Table Tree Treats Are Rooted in Swiftness

TREES traditionally take their own sweet time to grow. But producing these colorful candy versions will yield flavorful holiday table favors in only moments, assures Barbara Monderine-Anderson of East Rockaway, New York.

Making one requires just a few simple supplies—including a coffee mug, glue and wrapped candies. Even so, the trees will be savored for days by all ages. "Ours lasts well past the New Year," Barbara notes.

Materials Needed:
Coffee mugs—one metallic green and one white with holiday design or colors of choice
Two 6-inch-high plastic, cardboard or Styrofoam cones with a 3-inch base
Wrapped hard candies—two 10-ounce packages or about 100 peppermints and two 10-ounce packages or about 100 pieces of assorted candies
5/8-inch-wide gift ribbon—2 yards of green and 2 yards of red
1-inch gold plastic star

Lollipop
Scissors
Low-temperature glue gun and glue sticks

Finished Size: Each candy tree is about 12 inches tall x 5 inches wide, including mug handle.

Directions:
PEPPERMINT MUG: Starting about 1/2 in. from bottom of cone and using glue gun, glue end of candy wrappers, one at a time, to outside of cone, placing candies as close together as possible. Glue a second row of candy, centering it between two candies in previous row and overlapping first row of candies slightly. Continue gluing candies in place until entire cone is covered. Let glue dry.

Set candy-filled cone on top of green mug. Cut an 18-in. length of red gift ribbon. Set mug in center of ribbon. Bring ribbon ends to top of tree and tie snugly.

Repeat on other side with another 18-in. length of ribbon and tie as shown

in photo above. Cut remaining ribbon in half lengthwise and then into four equal pieces. Tie ribbons to top of tree. If desired, curl streamers by drawing ribbon across edge of scissors.

Glue gold star to top of candy tree.

ASSORTED CANDY MUG: Glue assorted candies to cone as directed for Peppermint Mug. Set candy-filled cone on top of Christmas design mug. Trim with green gift ribbon as directed above.

Insert lollipop stick into top of cone and glue into place. ❦

Wreath Motif Rounds Out Wardrobe

WHATEVER the occasion, this knit sweater makes merrily appropriate apparel. It works equally well for holiday parties *or* everyday attire, says Marion Kelley of Lansing, Michigan.

The wreath motif that gives this garment its seasonal feeling is a quick addition. "I used duplicate stitching to add it after I finished knitting," Marion relates. "It took no time at all."

Materials Needed:
Chart on next page
Worsted-weight yarn*—four 3-1/2-ounce skeins of green for body of sweater, 10 yards of bright red, 5 yards of white and 10 yards of light green for duplicate stitch design, 4 yards of bright yellow (or 12 inches of yellow ribbon or washable cord) for bow
Knitting needles—sizes 6 and 10 or size needed to obtain correct gauge
Four safety pins or stitch markers
Five 1-inch toggle buttons or any 3/4-inch to 1-inch novelty buttons
Size 18 tapestry needle
Scissors
*Marion used Coats and Clark Red Heart Classic yarn.

Finished Size: Directions are for an Adult size Medium with a garment chest measurement of about 42 inches and a garment length measurement of about 24 inches. Changes for sizes Small (38-1/2-inch chest and 22-inch length) and Large (47-inch chest and 26-inch length) are in parentheses.

Gauge: When working in St st on size 10 needles, 15 sts and 20 rows = 4 inches. To save time, take time to check gauge.

Stitches Used:
STOCKINETTE STITCH: St st
   Row 1 (RS): K across row.
   Row 2 (WS): P across row.
   Repeat Rows 1 and 2.
KNIT 1, PURL 1, RIBBING: k 1, p 1 rib
   Row 1: * K 1, p 1; repeat from * across row.
   Row 2: * P 1, k 1; repeat from * across row.

Directions:
BACK: With smaller needles and green, cast on 79(71,87) sts. Work k 1, p 1 rib for 2 in., inc 1 st on last row: 80(72,88) sts. Change to larger needles.

   Row 1: K across row.
   Row 2 and all even-numbered rows: P across row.
   Row 3: K across row.
   Row 5: K 7(3,11); * p 1, k 12; repeat from * to last 8(4,12) sts; p 1, k 7(3,11).
   Row 7: K 6(2,10); * p 3, k 10; repeat from * to last 9(5,13) sts; p 3, k 6(2,10).
   Row 9: Repeat Row 5.
   Rows 11-20: Repeat Rows 1 and 2.
   Repeat Rows 5-20 until piece measures 15(14,16)in. including the ribbing. Mark each end of row with safety pins or st markers for beginning of armholes. Continue working even in established pattern until armholes measure 9(8,10) in., ending with a WS row.
   Shape back neck as follows: Keeping in established pattern, work across 30(27,32) sts; attach a second skein and bind off center 20(18,24) sts; finish row

in established pattern. Working each side of neckline with its own skein of yarn, dec 1 st each neck edge every row 3 times. Bind off remaining 27(24,29) sts.
   FRONT: Work same as back until piece measures approximately 10(8,12) in., ending with a WS row.
   Shape front opening as follows: Keeping in established pattern, work across 38(34,42) sts; attach a second skein and bind off center 4 sts; finish row in established pattern. Working each side of front opening with its own skein of yarn, work even in established pattern until piece measures same as back to armholes.
   Mark each end of row with safety pins or st markers for beginning of armholes. Continue working even in established pattern until armholes measure

5(5,5) in., ending with a WS row.

Shape front neck as follows: Continuing to work each side off its own skein of yarn and keeping in established pattern, bind off 6(5,8) sts at beginning of neck edge. Dec 1 st at each neck edge every other row 5 times. Work even on remaining 27(24,29) sts until armholes measure same as back. Bind off all sts.

Sew shoulder seams using tapestry needle and matching yarn.

SLEEVE (Make two): With RS facing and larger needles, pick up 65(59, 71) sts evenly spaced between armhole markers. With WS facing, p across row.

Row 1: K across row.

Row 2 and all even-numbered rows: P across row.

Row 3: K across row.

Row 5: K 6(3,9); * p 1, k 12; repeat from * to last 7(4,10) sts; p 1, k 6(3,9).

Row 7: K 5(2,8); * p 3, k 10; repeat from * to last 8(5,11) sts; p 3, k 5(2,8).

Row 9: Repeat Row 5.

Rows 11-20: Repeat Rows 1 and 2.

Repeat Rows 5-20, keeping in established pattern until sleeve measures 2(2,2) in. Dec 1 st at each edge of next row. Allowing for decreased sts and continuing to work in established pattern, dec 1 st each edge every 5th row 11 times. Work even, keeping in established pattern on remaining 41(35,47) sts until sleeve measures 16(15-1/2,16-1/2) in.

Change to smaller needles. Work k 1, p 1 rib for 2 in. Bind off all sts.

LEFT FRONT RIBBING: With RS facing and smaller needles at left neck edge, pick up 53 sts evenly spaced along left front opening. Work k 1, p 1 rib for 6 rows. Bind off all sts in ribbing.

RIGHT FRONT RIBBING: With RS facing and smaller needles at bottom of right front opening, pick up 53 evenly spaced along right front opening.

Row 1: Work in k 1, p 1 rib to last st; k 1.

Row 2: Work in p 1, k 1 rib to last st; p 1.

Row 3: Work 2 sts in rib; * bind off 2 sts in rib, work 9 sts in rib; repeat from * three more times; bind off 2 sts in rib, work in rib to end.

Row 4: * Work in rib to bound-off sts, cast on 2 sts; repeat from * four more times, work in rib to end.

Rows 5-6: Repeat Rows 1 and 2.

Row 7: Bind off in rib.

NECK RIBBING: With RS facing and smaller needles, pick up 87(83,91) sts around neck edge. Work in k 1, p 1 rib for 4 rows. Bind off in rib.

DUPLICATE STITCHING: Following the color key and wreath motif chart, stitch design so it is centered around a purl stitch pattern (Fig. 1) on upper left front as shown in photo at left. See duplicate stitch illustration (Fig. 2).

Add French knots to holly using red yarn. See Fig. 3.

Finger-crochet two strands of yellow

yarn into a 12-in. cord. Knot or weave ends into cord to prevent raveling. Tie cord into bow around candy canes as shown in photo. Or tie purchased ribbon or cord into bow around candy canes and knot or trim ends at an angle to prevent raveling.

FINISHING: Using matching yarn, sew underarm seams. Sew ends at base of front opening to body of sweater. Sew buttons to left opening to correspond with buttonholes. 🍂

ABBREVIATIONS	
dec	decrease
inc	increase
k	knit
p	purl
RS	right side
st(s)	stitch(es)
WS	wrong side

Fig. 1 Purl stitch pattern

Fig. 2 Duplicate stitch

Fig. 3 French knot

WREATH MOTIF CHART

Stitch wreath motif centered around a purl stitch pattern on upper left side.

X = Center of chart

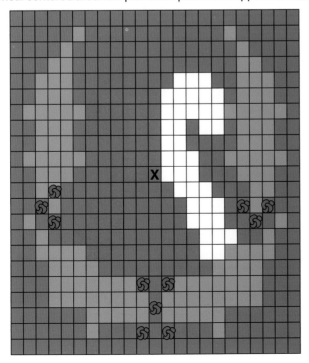

WREATH MOTIF COLOR KEY	
■	Red
□	White
■	Light green
🌀	French knot

'Chicken Scratch' Feathers Your Nest with Festiveness

IF YOU'RE ITCHING to get stitching trims for your tree, don't pass up this precious pair from Diane Oxner, Ocklawaha, Florida. She used a neat embroidery technique—chicken scratch—to fashion her designs.

Materials Needed (for both):
Charts on this page and the next page
1/8-inch check gingham fabric—two 9-inch squares each of green for Christmas tree and red for heart
Six-strand embroidery floss—green and red
Embroidery needle
Polyester stuffing
Glass seed beads—green for Christmas tree and red for heart
Beading needle
Embroidery hoop (optional)
1/2 yard of 1/4-inch-wide satin picot ribbon—green for Christmas tree and red for heart
Standard sewing supplies

Finished Size: Christmas tree trim is 4-1/2 inches across x 5 inches high. Heart trim is 5-1/2 inches across x 4 inches high.

Directions:
EMBROIDERY: Following charts, stitch Christmas tree design centered on one green gingham square and heart design

centered on one red gingham square. To find center of chart, draw lines across chart connecting arrows. Begin stitching at this point on appropriate color of gingham square.

Cut the six-strand floss into 18-in. lengths and use three strands for all stitching. Place fabric right side up in embroidery hoop if desired.

To start stitching, make a tight knot at the end of the floss and bring thread up from the back of the work in color of square indicated on chart. Stitch each piece using stitches indicated, pulling stitches taut but not so taut that the fabric puckers. See Fig. 1 and color and stitch keys. End floss by tying a knot in the back.

When stitching is complete, use one strand of floss to stitch green seed beads to Christmas tree trim and red seed beads to heart trim where shown on charts.

ASSEMBLY (for both): Place completed design on matching fabric with right sides together and edges matching. Machine-stitch around outside edge of design, 3/8 in. from stem stitching,

---

CHRISTMAS TREE COLOR AND STITCH KEY
- ✕ Green cross-stitches worked on medium checks only
- — Green straight stitches to form octagons
- ✳ Red double cross-stitches worked in centers of octagons
- ● Green seed beads
- – – Stem-stitch outline

CHRISTMAS TREE CHART

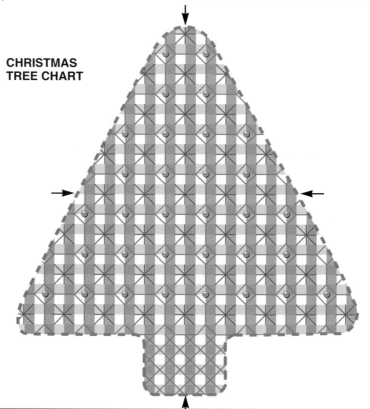

leaving an opening for turning. Trim seams and clip curves and corners. Turn right side out and stuff firmly. Turn raw edges of openings in and hand-stitch openings closed.

FINISHING: Cut an 8-in. piece of green ribbon and fold it in half. Stitch the ends together to the top of the Christmas tree to form a loop for hanging. Tie the remaining green ribbon into a bow and hand-stitch bow to top of tree over stitched ends of hanging loop. Repeat for heart, using red ribbon.

HEART COLOR AND STITCH KEY

× Red cross-stitches worked on light/medium rows of checks
— Red straight stitches radiating from a dark check, worked diagonally on white checks
● Red seed beads sewn on dark checks
-- Stem-stitch outline

CHICKEN SCRATCH TRIMS CHARTS

Note: Gingham fabric has light, medium and dark checks. The checks form two definite row variations—light/medium and medium/dark. Be sure to place stitches as shown on the charts as the stitch patterns are worked on specific rows to utilize these color values and enhance the light/dark effect of gingham.

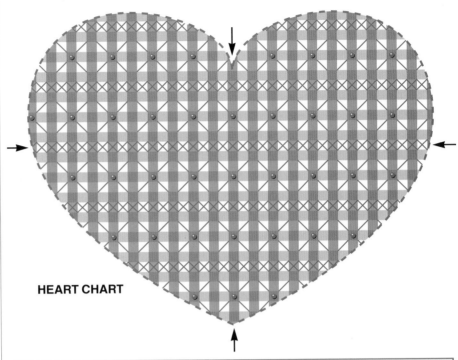

HEART CHART

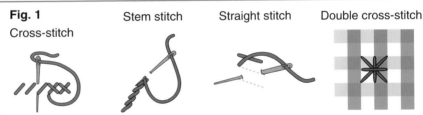

Fig. 1
Cross-stitch

Stem stitch

Straight stitch

Double cross-stitch

'Ageless' Snowflake's Easy Enough for a Child to Try

THE FLAKES will fly when you share this easy tree trim with youngsters!

It's uncomplicated enough for any age to tackle, confirms crafter Verlyn King of Tremonton, Utah. And because the supplies, including Popsicle sticks and pom-poms, are so simple to gather, it's ideal for group crafting as well.

Materials Needed:
Four craft sticks (Popsicle sticks)
White acrylic craft paint
Small paintbrush
Paper plate or palette
Crystal glitter
Nine 1/2-inch white pom-poms
Eight 1/4-inch white pom-poms

White tacky glue
White crochet cotton or thread for hanger

Finished Size: Snowflake measures 4 inches across.

Directions:
Place a small amount of white paint on paper plate or palette. Paint all sides of each craft stick white. Let dry.

Thin glue with water and apply to one side of each craft stick. While glue is still wet, sprinkle on glitter. Let dry.

Stack and glue the craft sticks in snowflake shape as shown in photo at right.

Glue a 1/2-in. pom-pom to center of stacked craft sticks and to both ends of

each craft stick. Glue 1/4-in. pom-poms to craft sticks around center pom-pom.

Cut a 5-in. piece of thread or crochet cotton and tie ends together. Glue loop to the end of one craft stick for hanger.

Cozy Up to Christmas with A Quick-to-Do Knit Blanket

NO ONE will mind if the weather outside is frightful…as long as this snuggly Yuletide blanket is nearby.

Avid knitter E.J. Slayton of Cadet, Missouri created the design to use for the holidays—and beyond. "The snowflake design makes it just right for wintry decorating," she tells. And, you can easily make it either an afghan or throw size because it is knit in strips.

Materials Needed:
Chart on this page
Worsted-weight yarn in 3-1/2-ounce skeins—8(15) skeins of green and one skein of white*
Size 6 (4mm) knitting needles or size needed to obtain correct gauge
Cable needle and stitch markers
Tapestry needle
Scissors

*E.J. used Brown Sheep Co. Inc. Nature Spun yarn, a 100% wool yarn sold in 3-1/2-ounce skeins with 245 yards/100 grams—approximately 8(15) skeins 1,960(3,675) yards of Monument Green #N27 and 1 skein of Natural #730.

Finished Size: Directions are for throw size, 42 inches x 46 inches. Changes for afghan size, 58 inches x 64 inches, are in parentheses.

Gauge: 20 sts and 28 rows = 4 inches in stockinette stitch.

Stitches Used:
STOCKINETTE STITCH: St st
Row 1 (RS): Knit across row.
Row 2 (WS): Purl across row.
Repeat Rows 1 and 2.
BACK CROSS (FRONT CROSS): BC (FC)
Slip next 3 sts to cable needle, hold in back (front), k 3, k 3 from cable needle.
MAKE 1: M 1
To increase one stitch, use left needle to pick up the horizontal strand between stitches, working from front to back. With right needle, knit in back of this stitch so it twists.
GARTER STITCH: Garter st
Every row: Knit across row.

Directions:
For throw size, make 3 inner strips and 1 left and 1 right strip. For afghan size make 5 inner strips and 1 left and 1 right strip.
INNER STRIP: Cast on 39 sts.
Bottom border: Work in garter st to make 6 ridges on RS, ending with a WS row.
Set-up row: K 1, p 1, [k 1, M 1] three times, p 1, place marker; k 3, M 1, [k 7, M 1] three times, k 3, place marker; p 1, [k 1, M 1] three times, p 1, k 1: 49 sts.
Rows 2, 4, 6 and 8 (WS): P 1, k 1, p 6, k 1; p 31; k 1, p 6, k 1, p 1.
Rows 3, 7 and 9 (RS): K 1, p 1, k 6, p 1; k 31; p 1, k 6, p 1, k 1.

Row 5: K 1, p 1, BC, p 1; k 31; p 1, FC, p 1, k 1.
Rows 10-57: Rep Rows 2-9 six more times, ending with Row 9.
Row 58: P 1, k 1, p 6; k 1; k 31; k 1; p 6, k 1, p 1.
Row 59: Rep Row 3.
Row 60: Rep Row 58.
Row 61: Rep Row 5.
Row 62: Rep Row 58.
Row 63: Rep Row 3.
Row 64: Rep Row 58.
Row 65: Rep Row 3.
Rep Rows 2-65 four (six) more times, making a total of five (seven) St st blocks, ending with Row 57 on fourth (sixth) repeat.
Decrease for top border: Decreasing 3 sts across 9 sts of each side border and 4 sts evenly across St st block, knit across next row. Work in garter st to make 5 ridges on RS, ending with a WS row. Bind off in purl on the RS.
Make a total of 3(5) inner strips.
RIGHT (LEFT) EDGE STRIP: Cast on 44 sts, work in garter st for 6 ridges on RS, ending with a WS row as for bottom border of inner strip. On set-up row, place marker 5 sts from right (left) edge. Keeping these 5 sts in garter st

DUPLICATE STITCH CHART

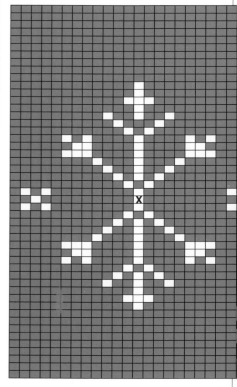

DUPLICATE STITCH KEY

X   Center of Row 29 of St st block
☐   Duplicate stitch

throughout, work right (left) edge strip on remaining 49 sts as for inner strip.

FINISHING: Using tapestry needle and green, stitch strips together, matching the cable crossings and stitching through Garter st "bumps" to make an almost invisible seam.

Following chart below left, use a single strand of white to duplicate-stitch snowflakes in the center of alternating blocks. See Fig. 1.

Weave in loose yarn ends and block if needed.

Fig. 1	Duplicate stitch

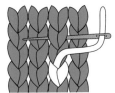

With tapestry needle and white, bring needle out at base of St stitch, then stitch under both legs of St stitch above, and stitch back into base.

ABBREVIATIONS

BC	back cross
FC	front cross
k	knit
p	purl
rep	repeat
RS	right side
st(s)	stitch(es)
WS	wrong side
[ ]	Instructions between brackets are repeated a given number of times.

Bovine Design Dispenses 'Moorriment'

BEEF UP your holiday decor with this clever cow-embellished wood stocking. It will hang nicely on a wall or a door…and lasso smiles aplenty! Patricia Schroedl put together the project for her Jefferson, Wisconsin home, but she notes that the stocking makes an appreciated present as well.

Materials Needed:

Patterns on pages 76 and 77
Tracing paper
Stylus or dry ballpoint pen
14 inches of 1 x 10 pine lumber (actual size about 3/4 inch x 9-1/4 inches)
4-inch square of 1/4-inch-thick basswood for cow cutout
Band or scroll saw
Router with round over bit (optional)
Sandpaper
Tack cloth
Drill with 1/4-inch bit
Palette or paper plate
Acrylic craft paints—black, bright blue, burgundy, dark green, ivory, light yellow, mint green, red, rose, soft blue and white*
Snow texture paint*
Paintbrushes—No. 4 and 8 flat, No. 4 round, No. 1 liner, 1-inch foam brush and old scruffy brush
1/2-inch copper cowbell
10 inches of 2-ply jute string
20 inches of twine
Toothpick
Wood glue
Black fine-line permanent marker
Acrylic spray varnish
*Patricia used DecoArt Snow-Tex and DecoArt Americana acrylic paints in True Red, Country Blue, Pineapple, Dusty Rose, Lamp Black, Victorian Blue, Burgundy Wine, Mint Julep Green, Titanium

White, Forest Green and Taffy Cream.

Finished Size: Stocking is 12-1/4 inches tall x 7 inches wide.

Directions:

Trace patterns on pages 76 and 77 onto tracing paper and cut out. Place pat-

(Instructions continue on next page)

terns on wood as directed and trace outlines with pencil.

Cut out stocking and cow using band or scroll saw. Round front edges of stocking with router or sandpaper. Drill hole where indicated on pattern. Sand stocking and cow until smooth. Wipe with tack cloth to remove sanding dust.

PAINTING: Place small amounts of paint on paper plate or palette as needed. Paint as directed below, continuing patterns around side edges. Apply a second coat as needed for complete coverage, allowing drying time between coats. Refer to photo on previous page and patterns on these pages for painting instructions as needed.

Stocking: Using the foam brush, basecoat body of stocking red and heel and toe soft blue. Apply snow texture paint to cuff of stocking using old scruffy brush.

Using appropriate size brush for each area, paint patches and stars as shown on pattern. Use handle of brush or toothpick to dab on paints to make dots, hearts and other small designs.

Wreath: Mix a few drops of dark green paint into about a teaspoon of snow texture paint. Use old scruffy brush to apply mixture to stocking for cow's wreath. Add a bit of plain snow texture randomly to wreath for snow.

Cow: Place pattern over cow cutout. Applying enough pressure to indent wood, use stylus or dry ballpoint pen to trace over inside pattern lines.

Using appropriate size brush for each area, paint cow as shown on pattern. Use handle of paintbrush to paint

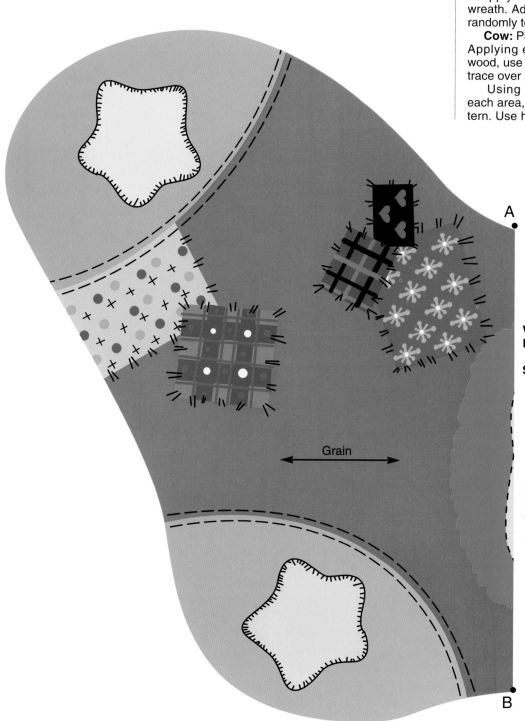

A

B

Grain

WOOD COW STOCKING PATTERNS

STOCKING
  Trace 1—tracing paper
  Cut 1—1 x 10 pine

Note: Trace stocking pattern onto tracing paper, joining the two pieces by matching dots A to A and B to B before cutting out.

nostrils and eyes black. Use flat brush and white to highlight cheeks.

Season's Mooings: Using liner brush or handle of paintbrush and black, paint "Season's Mooings" on cuff of stocking as shown on pattern. Use liner brush and dark green to paint holly leaves. Use toothpick and red to add berries to holly.

FINISHING: Glue cow to stocking where indicated on pattern.

Using marker, draw all "stitches" where indicated on pattern.

Spray stocking with sealer. Let dry.

Thread cowbell onto jute. Tie ends in bow and glue under cow's muzzle as shown in photo.

Thread twine through hole at top of stocking. Tie in bow and knot ends to prevent raveling.

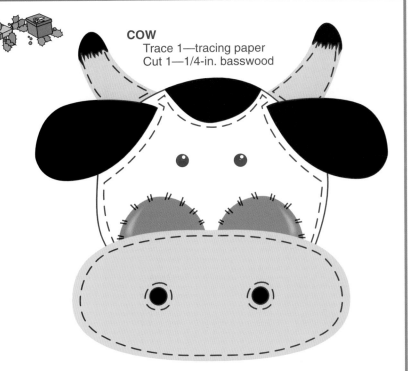

COW
Trace 1—tracing paper
Cut 1—1/4-in. basswood

A

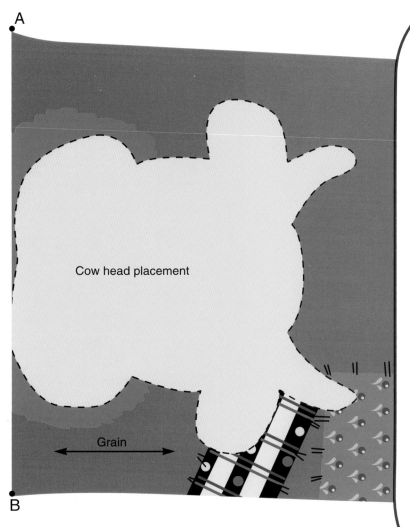

Cow head placement

Grain

B

Season's Mooings

Drill 1/4-in. hole here ➞

Quilted Casserole Cover Glows on the Outside, Too

THIS PIECEMEAL IDEA will keep your best recipes piping hot *and* brighten the tabletop at the same time. Plus, the cover takes the fuss out of carrying oven-baked dishes to Yule gatherings.

Gayla Cox of Guthrie, Oklahoma notes that salvaging penny-saving scraps from past projects to put together her casserole warmer makes it even more practical.

Materials Needed:
100% cotton or cotton-blend fabrics—
sixty-eight 3-inch squares to include green solids, red solids and assorted Christmas prints
3/4 yard of white terry cloth or one white terry cloth bath towel
3/4 yard of lightweight batting
Two red 20-inch zippers
Red all-purpose thread
One package of red double-fold bias tape
Standard sewing supplies

Finished Size: Casserole cover measures 10 inches wide x 15 inches long x 2-1/2 inches high and will fit over a standard 13-inch x 9-inch pan.

Directions:
Pre-wash all fabrics without fabric softeners, washing colors separately. If the water from any fabric is discolored, wash again until rinse water runs clear. Machine-dry and press all fabrics.

PIECING: Lay out fabric squares as shown in Fig. 1, taking care not to place similar or like fabrics next to each oth-er. Keeping rest of layout intact, pick up first horizontal row and stack squares in planned order.

With right sides together and an accurate 1/4-in. seam, sew the first two squares together. Next, add the third square. Continue to add squares until row is complete. Press seams in one direction.

In the same way, pick up and sew the next horizontal row. Press seams in opposite direction of first row. With right sides together, pin second row to the bottom edge of first row. Sew rows together, taking care to match corners of blocks. Press seam toward first row.

Continue to sew blocks and rows together in this way, following layout in Fig. 1 and pressing seams in alternating directions.

QUILTING: Lay terry cloth fabric or towel on a flat surface and smooth out all wrinkles. Place batting over terry cloth and smooth out. Place the pieced casserole cover right side up on top of batting. Pin all layers together. Cut out terry cloth and batting 1 in. beyond outside edges of cover.

Hand-baste through all three layers, stitching from center to corners, then horizontally and vertically every 4 in. until layers are held together. Using red thread, stitch-in-the-ditch of each seam. Trim batting and terry cloth even with outside edges of pieced cover.

FINISHING: Referring to Figs. 1 and 2, fold inside corner squares right sides together and stitch edges of corner squares together with a 1/4-in. seam, backstitching at the beginning and end of each seam.

With right sides together, stitch one long edge of binding to casserole cover lid, matching raw edges. Trim off excess. Repeat on bottom of casserole cover. Fold binding to inside and hand-stitch folded edge to terry cloth, covering seam. Remove basting thread.

Center and pin pull tab end of closed zipper right side up to one half of wrong side of casserole cover lid. Machine-stitch one edge of zipper to bias binding so teeth of zipper are just showing beyond bias tape as shown in Fig. 3.

Open zipper and stitch other edge of zipper tape to bottom of casserole cover. In the same way, stitch remaining zipper to other half of lid and bottom of casserole cover.

At base of zippers, where bottom and lid meet, hand-stitch across zipper teeth several times to hold the lid and bottom together. On inside, trim away excess zipper about 1/2 in. from stitching.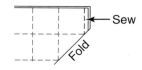

Fig. 1 Piecing layout

Lid

Inside corners

Bottom

Fig. 2
Bring right sides of squares together, matching raw edges, and machine-stitch using 1/4-in. seam allowance.

Sew

Fold

Fig. 3 Adding zippers

Zipper teeth
Zipper pull tabs
Lid lining
Zipper tape

Metal stopper
Lid
Zipper pull
Bottom
Zipper pull
Metal stopper

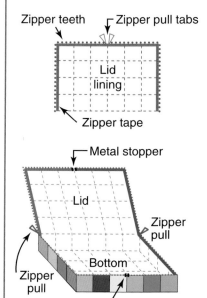

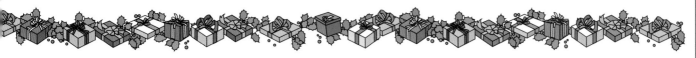

Novel Gift Takes Page from Practicality

HAVE a book lover on your Christmas list? Be practical—in a pretty way. Not only does this tote cover tomes in Christmas cheer, it sports helpful handles for easy carrying and a handy built-in bookmark, too.

Crafter Janna Britton of Firebaugh, California advises whipping up one for yourself as well as others for friends and family. "I use mine to hold a small notebook where I keep track of all our holiday plans," she details.

Materials Needed:

1/3 yard or 8-3/4-inch x 15-inch scrap of 100% cotton or cotton-blend plaid or Christmas print fabric
1/3 yard or 8-3/4-inch x 15-inch scrap of red felt
1/3 yard or 8-1/4-inch x 14-1/2-inch scrap of lightweight paper-backed fusible web
2 yards of 3/8-inch-wide red satin ribbon
Two small purchased wooden hearts
Red acrylic paint
1/2-inch flat paintbrush
DMC red (No. 666) six-strand embroidery floss
Fabric glue
Glue gun and glue sticks
Embroidery needle
Scissors
Straight pins

Finished Size: Book tote is 7-3/4 inches x 10 inches.

Directions:

Cut the following (if necessary): one 8-3/4-in. x 15-in. piece of plaid or Christmas print, one 8-1/4-in. x 14-1/2-in. piece of fusible web and one 8-3/4-in. x 15-in. piece of red felt.

Center fusible web on wrong side of plaid or Christmas print fabric and fuse into place, following manufacturer's directions. Remove paper backing and then fuse wrong side of fabric to felt, matching edges.

Trim fused piece to a 7-3/4-in. x 14-in. rectangle.

With felt side up, fold a 2-in. flap toward center of piece along each short edge and pin flaps in place. The piece should now measure 7-3/4 in. x 10 in.

Thread the embroidery needle with unseparated six-strand embroidery floss. Blanket-stitch (Fig. 1) along top and bottom edges of fused piece, making sure to stitch the top and bottom

edges of flaps to tote sides.

Pin ribbon to front of book tote as shown in Fig. 2. Glue ribbon in place, as positioned, using fabric glue. Tie ribbon ends into bow. Secure bow with a couple of hand-stitches. Cut ribbon ends at an angle to desired length.

BOOKMARK: Paint wooden hearts red and let dry.

Cut a 12-in. piece of ribbon. Using glue gun, glue one end of ribbon between two wood hearts with edges matching and ribbon extending from top of hearts as shown in photo above.

Place other end of ribbon at center

top of felt side of cover. Glue 2 in. of ribbon onto felt. Secure ribbon with a couple of hand-stitches.

Fig. 1
Blanket stitch

Fig. 2
Positioning ribbon handle

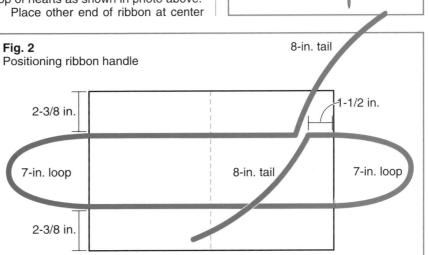

8-in. tail

2-3/8 in.

1-1/2 in.

7-in. loop

8-in. tail

7-in. loop

2-3/8 in.

Jumper's Flavored with Gingerbread

GRINS GALORE are what you will pocket when you stitch this goody-filled garment for your favorite little miss.

Take your pick of approaches to the project. You can embellish an already-made jumper with the gingerbread men pockets if you like. Or, as an alternative, use a store-bought pattern like Avon Mackay of Waukesha, Wisconsin did in creating the craft.

Materials Needed:
Patterns on next page
Tracing or pattern paper
Pencil
Red jumper*
100% cotton or cotton-blend fabrics—
*   1/3 yard each of dark tan for gingerbread shapes and red plaid for bows and scrap of red solid for cheeks and hearts*
1/3 yard of paper-backed fusible web
1/3 yard of tear-away stabilizer or typing paper
Red all-purpose thread
Six-strand embroidery floss—red and black
Size 6 embroidery needle
Iron and ironing surface
Scissors
Standard sewing supplies
*Commercial jumper patterns similar to the one Avon used are available.

Finished Size: Gingerbread shape is 9-1/2 inches tall x 6-1/2 inches wide and will fit on almost any Child size garment. The design may be enlarged or reduced on a copy machine to fit other size garments as well.

Directions:
Fold tracing paper in half. With fold of paper matching foldline of pattern, trace pattern. Cut out pattern and unfold paper to complete the pattern.

Cut two 10-1/2-in. x 14-1/2-in. pieces of dark tan fabric and one 10-in. x 14-in. piece of fusible web. Center fusible web on wrong side of one dark tan fabric piece and fuse together following manufacturer's directions. Remove paper backing and fuse to wrong side of matching fabric piece.

Trace two gingerbread shapes onto fused fabric, matching grainlines. Cut out on traced lines.

Trace four hearts and four cheeks onto the paper side of a small piece of fusible web. Fuse web onto wrong side of red fabric. Cut out shapes and remove paper backing. Fuse hearts and cheeks onto one side of each gingerbread shape where indicated on pattern.

EMBROIDERY: Separate six-strand floss and use three strands for all embroidery. Referring to pattern for placement, make a black French knot for each eye and red stem stitches for each mouth (Fig. 1).

APPLIQUEING: Before attaching gingerbread shapes to garment, satin-stitch around each shape using red thread and a medium satin stitch. Referring to applique key, stitch again around outside edges of heads (between dots) using red thread and a wide satin stitch.

Stitch around cheeks and hearts using red thread and a medium satin stitch.

Referring to the photo above left for placement, pin gingerbread shapes to garment. Place stabilizer or typing paper behind appliques.

Using wide satin stitch and red thread, stitch gingerbread shapes to garment, stitching between dots around body of gingerbread shape and leaving space between dots at top of head open.

To create each pocket, straight-stitch through all thicknesses at gingerbread

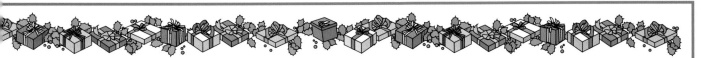

men's necks where indicated on pattern.

Remove stabilizer and pull all loose threads to back and secure.

FINISHING: Cut two 12-in. x 1-in. bias strips from red plaid fabric. Fold each in half lengthwise with right sides together and stitch long edges with a scant 1/4-in. seam. Turn each right side out through one end and press. Knot the ends and make two bows. Hand-stitch bows to gingerbread shapes where indicated on pattern.

APPLIQUE KEY

—·—· Wide satin-stitch applique only

— — — Wide satin-stitch applique to garment

— — Straight-stitch applique to garment

Fig. 1

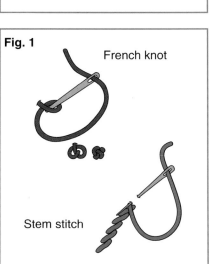

French knot

Stem stitch

CHEEK
Trace 4—fusible web
Cut 4—red solid

HEART
Trace 4—fusible web
Cut 4—red solid

GINGERBREAD PATTERNS

GINGERBREAD POCKET
Trace 1—folded tracing paper
Cut 2—fused dark tan fabric

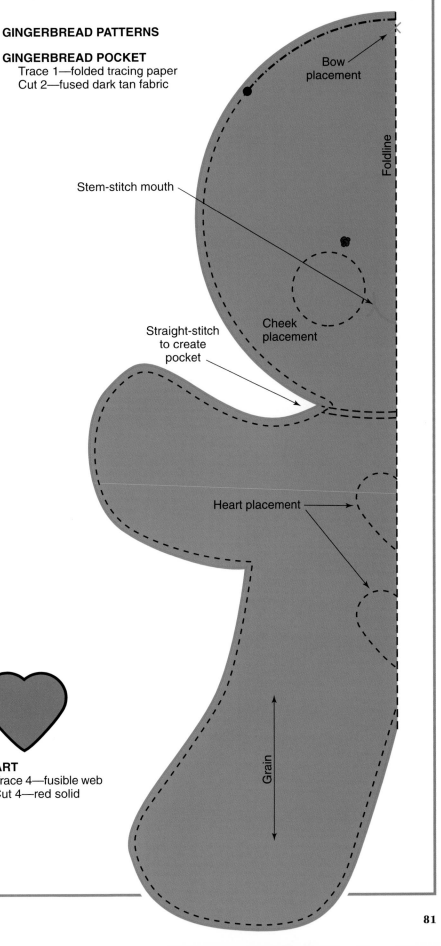

Bow placement

Foldline

Stem-stitch mouth

Cheek placement

Straight-stitch to create pocket

Heart placement

Grain

Merry Pair Lends Apparel a Timely Air

FEATURING Santa Claus and his kindly missus, this easy-to-bead wooden necklace will turn any top from your closet into a pretty seasonal sight.

Attests Betty Souther of Dos Palos, California, "The necklace goes with just about everything. I've given quite a few as gifts and taken more to craft fairs. It always proves popular."

Materials Needed:

Patterns on next page
Tracing paper
2-inch x 12-inch piece of 1/4-inch-thick basswood
Scroll or band saw
Drill with 1/8-inch bit
Sandpaper
Tack cloth
1 yard of 1/8-inch-wide green satin ribbon
Red round wood beads—twenty-one 10mm and two 5mm*
Paintbrushes—No. 4 flat, No. 1 round or fine liner and old scruffy brush or toothbrush
Stylus or dry ballpoint pen
Acrylic craft paints—black, dark green, flesh, grey, ivory, red and white**
Water-base satin varnish
Black fine-line permanent marker
Palette or paper plate

*Red wood beads are available at most craft stores. Or you can paint natural wood beads red.
**Betty used Delta Ceramcoat paints in Bright Red, White, Black, Ivory, Christmas Green, Flesh Medium and Drizzle Grey.

Finished Size: Design area of necklace is 14 inches long. Wood cutouts are 1-5/8 inches to 2-1/4 inches tall x 1-1/4 inches across.

Directions:

Trace patterns on next page onto tracing paper and cut out. Trace around patterns onto wood as directed and cut out, using scroll or band saw. Drill holes where directed on patterns. Sand pieces to smooth rough edges and wipe with tack cloth to remove sanding dust.

Using flat brush, apply varnish to wood cutouts to seal wood and give a smoother painting surface. When dry, sand gently and wipe again with tack cloth.

PAINTING: Paint all sides of cutouts and extend designs around sides. Apply additional coats as needed for complete coverage and allow drying time between each coat.

Using flat brush, basecoat trees green and Santa and Mrs. Santa red.

Let all pieces dry.

Transfer detail lines onto shapes by placing patterns over cutouts and tracing over detail lines with stylus or dry ballpoint pen, applying enough pressure to indent wood. Referring to patterns and painting diagrams at right, paint details onto cutouts, using appropriate color paint and type of brush for each area.

Trees: Referring to painting pattern and photo at left, use flat brush and thinned white to paint scallops on trees. Let dry.

Place trees on newspaper to protect surfaces around and underneath them. Mix about 1/2 teaspoon of white paint with 1/2 teaspoon of water. Dip old brush or toothbrush into thinned paint. Hold bristles about 8 in. from trees and pull another brush handle or your finger across the bristles to spatter trees. Repeat until desired effect is achieved. Let dry.

Santa: Referring to painting pattern, use flat brush to paint face flesh, beard, mustache, eyebrows and hair ivory, trim on hat and jacket grey, mittens green and boots black. Let dry.

Use white and nearly dry brush to paint over grey trim on Santa's hat and jacket to create a "fur" look.

Dip handle of brush or toothpick into black to paint eyes. Use red in the same manner to paint Santa's nose and mouth.

Mrs. Santa: Referring to painting pattern and photo, use flat brush to paint Mrs. Santa's face and hands flesh, hair ivory and apron and cuffs of dress white.

Dip handle of brush or toothpick into red to paint heart on Mrs. Santa's apron. In the same manner, use white to make dots around apron.

Use liner brush to paint mouth red and stripes on Mrs. Santa's apron red and green.

FINISHING: Use black marker to add details on Santa and Mrs. Santa as shown on patterns.

Use red paint and a nearly dry brush to add blush to cheeks of Santa and Mrs. Santa.

When dry, use flat brush to apply varnish to all sides of painted cutouts.

Thread beads and cutouts on ribbon in order shown in photo and center them on ribbon. Tie overhand knot close to outside beads. Trim ends of ribbon to desired length and knot or cut ends at an angle to prevent raveling.

NECKLACE PATTERNS AND PAINTING DIAGRAMS

SANTA
Trace 1—tracing paper
Cut 1—1/4-in. basswood

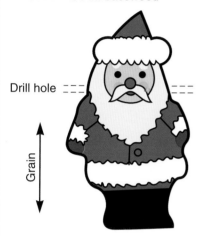

Drill hole
Grain

MRS. SANTA
Trace 1—tracing paper
Cut 1—1/4-in. basswood

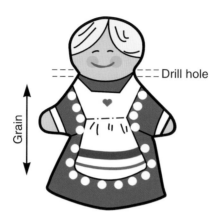

Drill hole
Grain

TREE
Trace 1—tracing paper
Cut 4—1/4-in. basswood

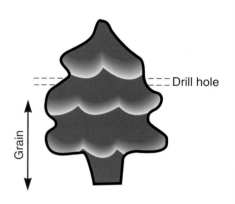

Drill hole
Grain

Eye-Catching Booties Are in Step with Season

INSPIRED by Santa's snug footwear, Cherie Marie Leck of Charlotte, North Carolina crocheted infant-sized replicas sure to warm a baby's toes—and the heart of anyone who sees them.

Don't limit the booties to children, though. They can be incorporated into a garland or even filled with candy and offered to friends and family!

Materials Needed:
Sport-weight yarn—small amounts or one skein each of red and white
Size G/6 (4.25mm) crochet hook
Safety pin

Finished Size: Booties will fit newborns to 6-month-old infants.

Gauge: With size G hook in sc, Rounds 1-3 (sole) = 3 inches long and 1-1/2 inches wide.

Special Stitches: DOUBLE CROCHET TWO STITCHES TOGETHER (dc 2 sts tog): Leave first dc unfinished with two lps remaining on the hk. Work the second dc until there are three lps on the hk, yo and complete both stitches as one by pulling through all lps on the hk at once.

Directions (make two):
Round 1 (sole): With red yarn, ch 8, sc in second ch from hk and next 5 chs, work 5 sc in end ch. Working on op-posite side of ch, sc in next 5 chs; work 2 sc in last ch: 18 sts. Mark last st with a safety pin. At the end of each round move this pin to the last st.

Round 2: Sc in next 6 sts; work 2 sc in each of next 5 sts; sc in next 6 sts; work 2 sc in next st: 24 sts.

Round 3: Sc in next 9 sts; work 2 sc in each of next 4 sts; sc in next 10 sts; work 2 sc in last st: 29 sts.

Rounds 4-5: Sc in each st around: 29 sts.

Round 6: Sc in next 10 sts; [dc 2 sts tog] four times; sc in next 11 sts: 25 sts.

Round 7: Sc in next 8 sts; [dc 2 sts tog] four times; sc in next 9 sts: 21 sts.

Round 8: Sc in next 8 sts; [dc 2 sts tog] twice; sc in next 9 sts; join with sl st in first sc: 19 sts.

Rounds 9-12: Ch 3 (counts as first dc here and throughout), dc in each st around; join with sl st to top of beginning ch-3: 19 sts. Fasten off at the end of Round 12.

Round 13: Join white in top of be-ginning ch-3, ch 3; dc in each st around; join with sl st to top of beginning ch-3: 19 sts.

Round 14: Ch 3, dc in each st around; join with sl st to top of beginning ch-3: 19 sts.

Round 15: Ch 1, sc in same st as sl st; sc in each st around; join with sl st in first sc. Fasten off. Turn down cuff. 🦌

ABBREVIATIONS
ch	chain
dc	double crochet
hk	hook
lp(s)	loop(s)
sc	single crochet
sl st	slip stitch
st(s)	stitches(s)
tog	together
yo	yarn over
[ ]	Instructions between brackets are repeat-ed a given number of times

Generous Knit Stocking Is Sized Right for the Holidays

IN KEEPING with the spirit of the season, Louise Purpura's stocking holds plenty of sentiment—and an extra helping of holiday treats, too.

"This one is a bit larger than others I've stitched, so it'll hold lots of goodies," agrees this Valparaiso, Indiana crafter. But more is less in another respect, she adds: "The stocking is fairly simple to finish, especially for folks who've done some knitting before."

Materials Needed:

Chart and pattern on next page
Worsted-weight yarn in 4-ounce (115-gram) skeins—one each of green, red and white
Knitting needles—pair of straight and set (four needles) of double-pointed in size 8 (5mm) or size needed to obtain correct gauge
Stitch holders—two small, one large
Stitch marker
Size C/2 (2.75mm) crochet hook
Tapestry needle
3/4 yard of 44-inch-wide 100% cotton or cotton-blend fabric for lining
Matching all-purpose thread
Small jingle bell (optional)
Standard sewing supplies

Finished Size: Stocking is about 22 inches long.

Gauge: When working in St st, 16 sts and 24 rows = 4 inches.

KNITTING REMINDERS:

Changing colors: To avoid holes when changing colors, always pick up new color of yarn from beneath dropped yarn.

Working in rounds: Place sts evenly on 3 dp needles. Place a marker at beginning of round, moving marker with each round worked. Being careful not to twist sts, join last st to first st by pulling up yarn firmly and making first st with fourth needle.

Stockinette stitch: St st
  Row 1 (RS): Knit across row.
  Row 2 (WS): Purl across row.
  Repeat Rows 1 and 2.
K 2, p 2 ribbing:
  Every Row: K 2, p 2 across row.

Directions:

With straight knitting needles and green, cast on 68 sts.
  Rows 1-10: Work in k 2, p 2 ribbing: 68 sts.

Rows 11-12: With red, work in St st.
Rows 13-16: With green, work in St st.
Rows 17-36: Working in St st and using colors shown in chart and listed on color key, follow Peace 1998 Chart on next page, starting at bottom of chart. Read chart from right to left for a knit row and from left to right for a purl row.
Rows 37-38: With red, work in St st.
Rows 39-40: With green, work in St st.
Rows 41-80: Using green and white yarns, work snowflake pattern on next page across rows, repeating Rows 1-8 five times, and dec 1 st at beginning and end of each Row 6.
Rows 81-84: Using green and white yarns, work Rows 1-4 of snowflake pattern.
Rows 85-86: With red, work in St st: 58 sts.
Rows 87-88: With green, work in St st.
Top of foot: Row 89: K 45, sl last 13 sts on small holder for heel.
Row 90: P 32, sl last 13 sts on second small holder for heel.
Rows 91-102: Work in St st on 32 sts. Slip sts onto large holder.
HEEL: Rows 1-11: Slip 13 sts of each side of heel from holders onto one dp needle so that the ends of the rows are at middle of needle. With RS facing, work in St st on 26 sts for 11 rows.
Turning heel: Row 12: P 15, p 2 tog, p 1, turn.
Heel Row 13: Sl 1, k 5, sl 1, k 1, psso, k 1, turn.
Heel Row 14: Sl 1, p 6, p 2 tog, p 1, turn.
Heel Row 15: Sl 1, k 7, sl 1, psso, k 1, turn.
Heel Row 16: Sl 1, p 8, p 2 tog, p 1, turn.
Heel Rows 17-22: Continue in this way, working out toward sides of heel and always working 1 more st before each dec on every row until 16 sts remain.
Heel Row 23: Join green at top right-hand side of heel: Pick up and k 12 sts along side of heel, k 16 sts of heel, pick up and k 12 sts along remaining side of heel: 40 sts.
Heel Row 24: P across row.
Heel Row 25: K 1, sl 1, k 1, psso, k to last 3 sts, k 2 tog, k 1.
Heel Rows 26-37: Repeat Rows 24 and 25: 26 sts.
FOOT: Round 1: (See knitting reminders for working in rounds.) Sl last

13 sts just worked from straight needle onto first dp needle. On second needle, k across 32 sts on holder; on third needle, k remaining 13 sts. Center of heel is now at beginning of each round: 58 sts.
Rounds 2-14: K each round.
Toe Shaping: Round 15: Change to red, on first needle, k to last 3 sts, k 2 tog, k 1; on second needle, k 1, sl 1, k 1, psso, k to last 3 sts, k 2 tog. On third needle, k 1, sl 1, k 1, psso, k to end of round.
Round 16: Knit.
Repeat Rounds 15 and 16 until there are 4 sts on each needle, ending with first needle. Break off yarn, leaving a 12-in. end. Run end through all sts, drawing up tightly.
FINISHING: Using tapestry needle and matching yarn, sew back seam and sides of instep.
Hanging Loop: Using any color yarn, ch 27. Fasten off, leaving an 8-in. yarn end. Fold chain in half and use yarn end to stitch both ends of chain to back seam at top edge of stocking.
Lining: Fold lining fabric with right sides together. Lay knitted stocking on top of fabric. Cut around stocking 1/2 in. from all edges. With right sides together, machine-stitch 1/2 in. from the edges, leaving top edge open.

Fold 2 in. of top edge to wrong side for hem. Trim hem to 1/2 in. from fold. With lining wrong side out, put lining inside stocking, positioning the top edge of lining 1-1/2 in. from top edge of stocking. Add jingle bell between layers if desired, working it down to tip of toe. Use matching thread to hand-stitch top edge of lining to inside of stocking. 🌿

SNOWFLAKE PATTERN

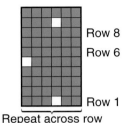

Row 8
Row 6

Row 1

Repeat across row

STOCKING COLOR KEY
■ Green
□ White

ABBREVIATIONS

ch	chain
dec	decrease
dp	double-pointed
k	knit
p	purl
psso	pass the slipped stitch over
RS	right side
sl	slip
st(s)	stitch(es)
tog	together
WS	wrong side

PEACE 1998 CHART

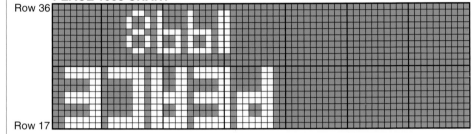

Row 36

Row 17

With No-Sew St. Nick, Neat Napkins Are at Hand

SANTA will run rings around your Christmas table when you fashion these festive felt napkin holders! The no-sew project is simple to complete—just cut out the pieces and glue them together.

Priscilla Weaver of Hagerstown, Maryland created the jolly fellow as a table favor for a holiday banquet. "Not many people used their napkins that night," she recalls. "I got so many compliments on the rings."

Materials Needed:
Patterns on this page

Tracing paper and pencil
Transparent tape or straight pins
5-inch square of white felt
Felt scraps—white, light pink, deep rose, light blue and red
White construction paper
Scissors
Tacky (white) glue
Red paper or cloth dinner napkin

Finished size: Each napkin ring is about 3-1/2 inches x 4 inches.

Directions:
Trace patterns at right onto tracing paper, tracing a separate pattern for each piece. Cut out. Tape or pin patterns to appropriate colors of felt and cut out. Referring to photo at left for placement, glue eyes, nose, cheeks and mouth onto pink face piece. Let dry. Glue face to hair/beard piece. Let dry.

Glue the eyebrows above eyes. Referring to photo, glue Santa's mustache so it partially covers his cheeks and mouth.

Cut a strip of white construction paper 1/2 in. wide x 9 in. long. Fold strip into thirds

and glue the overlapped ends together to form a ring that is approximately 3 in. wide. Let dry.

Center and glue ring to back of completed Santa. Let dry.

Fold a cloth or paper napkin as desired and slip it into the ring. 🌿

Note: Dashed lines indicate that piece is overlapped by another piece.

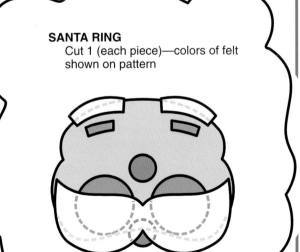

SANTA RING
Cut 1 (each piece)—colors of felt shown on pattern

Branch Out with a Beautiful Basket

MAKE THE MOST of your mantel this Christmas…by topping it with Gerda Shebester's bright basket.

With its evergreen embellishments, it'll spruce up the fireplace—or *any* surface. And, thanks to its narrow width, the basket's also ideal for hanging on a wall, reveals Gerda from her Milan, Michigan home.

Materials Needed:
Natural reed—1/2-inch flat for weavers, 5/8-inch flat for inside rim, 5/8-inch flat oval for outside rim, 1-inch flat for stakes, cane or 1/4-inch flat oval for lashing and No. 2 or 3 natural round for twining under the rim
Red-dyed reed—5/8-inch flat for weavers, No. 3 or 4 round for twining the base and 11/64-inch flat oval for curls*
Green-dyed reed—5/8-inch flat for weavers, 7/8-inch flat for stakes and No. 2 or 3 round to attach trees*
Five wood Christmas trees—1/4 inch thick x 1-1/2 inches high
Drill with 1/8-inch bit
Dark green acrylic paint or stain
Small paintbrush
Soft cloth or paper towel

Two 3/4-inch-wide wood ears (loops for hanging)
Sea grass for rim filler
Heavy scissors or side cutters
Tape measure
Pencil
Large plastic bucket to soak reed
Old towel
Spring-type clothespins
Craft glue
Needle-nose pliers
Natural or artificial Christmas greens and your choice of other decorations to fill basket (Gerda used artificial pine garland, red carnations, apple picks, twigs, cardinals and red velvet ribbon to decorate her basket)
Styrofoam—1-1/2-inch x 29-inch piece or scraps to fit inside basket

*To dye your own materials, use red and green Rit dye and follow the instructions included in the package.

Finished Size: Basket is 31 inches long x 1-7/8 inches wide at its base x 6-1/2 inches high.

Directions:
Drill hole through each tree from center top to center bottom. See Fig. 1. Paint or stain trees green and wipe while still wet so grain shows and finish is dulled.

For stakes, cut one 50-in. length and fifteen 22-in. lengths of 1-in. flat natural reed and four 22-in. lengths of 7/8-in. flat green reed. Soak reed in warm water until pliable, soaking dyed reed separately. Measure and mark the centers on the 22-in. stakes. Mark the center on the 50-in. center stake and also measure and mark points 15-1/2 in. from each side of the center mark.

Place towel on a flat surface. Lay out the 50-in. stake horizontally with a 22-in. natural stake centered under it. Referring to Fig. 2, lay out the stakes, spacing them 5/8 in. apart.

Twining the base: Soak the red round reed. Place ends of piece together to find center. Use needle-nose pliers to make a crimp about 12 in. from center. Loop the crimped spot around one of the stakes. Begin twining with the longer end, taking it over one stake and under the next. See Fig. 3. Twine around base with red for two rows.

Upsetting the stakes: Working with dampened basket base, gently bend each stake upward from the base by rolling stakes over your finger. Hold stakes in place with clothespins as needed.

SIDES: Cut one 70-in.-long weaver in colors indicated for each row. Soak weavers until pliable, soaking dyed reeds separately. Start each row on a

different side from last row, alternating over/under and under/over patterns. Keep stakes vertical and pack weaving down closely after each row, making sure that all sides of basket are the same height. Remove clothespins as you weave, replacing them if needed.

Rows 1-2: Beginning with natural 1/2-in. flat reed, position the end of the reed on the outside of one stake. Weave one row around the basket, alternating under and over stakes. When beginning stake is reached, continue under and over next few stakes, clipping the end of the weaver in the middle of the stake.

Row 3: Weave using 5/8-in. flat green reed.

Row 4: Weave using 5/8-in. flat red reed.

Row 5: Repeat Row 3.
Row 6: Repeat Row 4.

Insert an 8-in. length of green round reed through drilled hole of each tree. Referring to Fig. 4, set trees on top of Row 4 on the front of the basket at stakes 5, 7, 13 and 15. Place remaining tree on top of Row 5 at stake 10.

Row 7: Repeat Row 3.

Rows 8-9: Repeat Rows 1-2, overlapping green round reed above trees.

Insert wood ears on the outside of the basket at back stakes 5 and 15.

Rows 10-11: Twine with No. 2 or 3 natural round reed.

Top row finishing: Cut all inside stakes even with top. Bend all outside stakes to inside and secure behind weaving, using awl to open spaces as needed.

To maintain shape of basket, hold sides of basket together using scrap reed, inserting pieces from front to back. Let dry.

RIM: Soak 5/8-in. natural flat oval reed for outside of rim, 5/8-in. natural flat for inside of rim and sea grass filler. Measure inside and outside circumference of top and add 1-1/2 in. to measurements. Cut inside and outside reeds and sea grass to these measurements.

Securing rims with clothespins, wrap the flat oval reed around the outside. Cut ends at an angle and butt angled ends. Place flat reed on the inside of rim, cutting and butting ends in the same way.

Beginning on inside of basket, lash rim with soaked cane or 1/4-in. flat oval reed, placing sea grass between inside and outside rims and over stakes for filler. See Fig. 5.

FINISHING: Referring to photo, loop red 11/64-in. flat oval reed through alternating red and green flat reeds on each end of basket to create curls. Place Styrofoam inside basket and insert greens and other decorations. 🌿

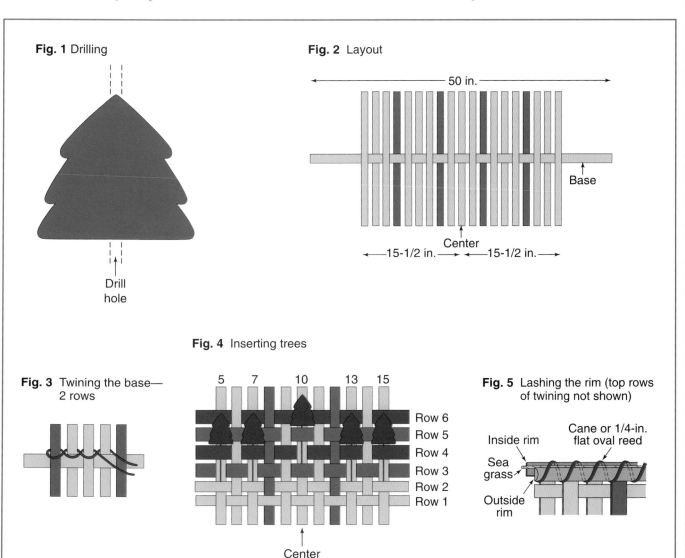

Fig. 1 Drilling

Drill hole

Fig. 2 Layout

50 in.

Base

Center

15-1/2 in.   15-1/2 in.

Fig. 3 Twining the base— 2 rows

Fig. 4 Inserting trees

5   7   10   13   15

Row 6
Row 5
Row 4
Row 3
Row 2
Row 1

Center

Fig. 5 Lashing the rim (top rows of twining not shown)

Inside rim

Sea grass

Outside rim

Cane or 1/4-in. flat oval reed

Homespun Mini-Quilts Can Trim Tree or Protect Table

Finished Size: Nine-patch ornaments are 4 inches square and 12-patch ornaments are 5 inches square.

Directions:

Pre-wash, dry and press all of the fabrics, if desired.

Do all piecing with accurate 1/4-in. seams and right sides of fabric together. Press seams toward darker fabrics when possible, unless directed otherwise.

Cut fabrics using rotary cutter and quilter's ruler or use water-soluble marker and ruler to mark fabrics and cut with scissors.

NINE-PATCH ORNA-MENT: For each nine-patch pieced top, cut the following: One 2-1/2-in. square from small print or stripe for center patch, four 1-1/2-in. squares from fabric of choice for corner patches and four 2-1/2-in. x 1-1/2-in. rectangles from contrasting fabric.

Arrange pieces as shown in Fig. 1 and stitch together, forming three rows. Stitch the three rows together to form a nine-patch square as shown in Fig. 1 and photo above.

TWELVE-PATCH ORNAMENT: For each 12-patch pieced top, cut the following: Four 1-3/4-in. squares from small plaid fabric, four 1-3/4-in. squares from small checked fabric (for center four-patch and corner patches) and four 3-in. x 1-3/4-in. rectangles from striped fabric as shown in photo above.

Arrange center squares as shown in Fig. 2 and stitch together, forming pieced center patch. Assemble three rows as shown in Fig. 1, using pieced center patch for center square. Stitch the three rows together to form 12-patch square as shown in photo.

FINISHING (for both): Using the pieced block as a pattern, cut quilt batting and muslin for backing.

Place muslin backing and pieced block right sides together on a flat surface. Place quilt batting on top. Pin all three layers together with edges matching. Backstitching at beginning and end of seam, machine-stitch around outside edges, leaving an opening for turning. Remove pins and clip corners diagonally. Turn right side out so batting is on the inside. Turn raw edges of opening in and hand-stitch closed.

Stitch buttons to center squares as shown in photo. Using contrasting embroidery floss or yarn, stitch an "X" at each intersection where corners meet.

Sew ends of satin ribbon together and hand-stitch to back edge of one corner for hanging loops if desired. 🍃

DOUBLE your Christmas decorating enjoyment—on the double.

These pleasing patchwork pieces stitch up speedily, according to Naomi Sebourn of Sarasota, Florida, and are equally at home hanging on the holiday tree *or* serving as clever coasters for a festive family function.

Materials Needed:

Scraps of 100% cotton or cotton-blend fabrics in colors of your choice to include small checks, plaids, stripes and prints
Small amount of lightweight cotton yarn or embroidery floss in colors to complement fabrics
1/8-inch-wide satin ribbon—one 3-inch length for each ornament in color of choice (for optional hanger)
Assorted buttons
Scrap of lightweight quilt batting
Scrap of unbleached muslin
Scissors
Rotary cutter and mat (optional)
Quilter's ruler
Water-soluble marker (optional)
Standard sewing supplies

Fig. 1
Row assembly for Nine-Patch Ornament

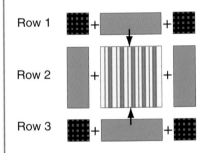

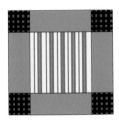

Fig. 2
Pieced center patch assembly for 12-Patch Ornament using 1-3/4-in. squares

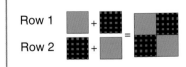

Pieced center patch

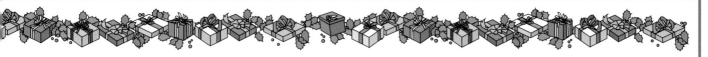

Lively Yuletide Takes Shape with North Pole Pals

FIGURING merriment into the season is truly a treat with this holly-jolly pair. You shape them from clay.

The Santa and elf fit perfectly on a mantel or a shelf. What's more, says Karen Taylor of Redding, California, her characters are good projects for youngsters to lend a helping hand with or even to tackle themselves.

Material Needed (for both):
Patterns on this page
Tracing paper and pencil
Oven-bake polymer clay—one package
*   each of white, flesh, yellow, red and*
*   green**
Waxed paper
Craft knife
Rolling pin
Brown paper grocery sack
Transparent tape
Scissors
Round toothpick
Four black seed beads for eyes
Scrap of cardboard or cutting board
Small paintbrush (optional)
Polymer clay glaze (optional)
*Karen used Sculpey III.

Finished Size: Santa and elf are each about 4-1/2 inches tall.

Directions: Knead clay until soft and smooth, making sure to wash hands each time you use a new color of clay.

Use rolling pin to roll out clay between sheets of waxed paper. Lay clay, still on waxed paper, on a cutting board or piece of cardboard when cutting out pieces. When joining pieces, work clay together with a knife or press into place firmly to avoid having pieces come apart.

Trace patterns above right onto tracing paper and cut out.

Trace around cone pattern onto grocery sack twice, cut out and form into two sharply pointed cones. Tape overlapping edges to hold in place.

SANTA: Roll out red to 1/8-in. thickness for body. Wrap around cone to cover, trimming as needed. Smooth seam with fingers.

From red, make two 1/2-in. balls and shape into arms as shown in photo at right. Press firmly onto each side of body and use toothpick and fingers to flatten and blend into body at top of cone.

Roll two 1/4-in. balls of white and press onto body at end of arms for hands.

From flesh, make a 7/8-in.-diameter

ball. Press down over point of cone for head.

From white, roll several very thin cylinders for hair and beard. Cut cylinders into short lengths and press against head as shown in photo. Form two very small balls of white into two mustache shapes and press in place over beard at center front. Use a toothpick to indent "whiskers" as shown in photo.

Roll a tiny ball of red and press between and a bit below mustache pieces for mouth.

Use toothpick to press two seed beads into face for eyes.

For hat, roll a 3/4-in. to 1-in. ball of red. Make a depression in ball to fit around head, then fashion into hat shape as shown in photo. Place on top of head and use a toothpick to press edge of hat in place. Add a 1/4-in. ball of white to point of cap. Roll a small cylinder of white to fit around base of hat. Flatten cylinder and press in place over base of hat for "fur" trim.

From white, roll an 1/8-in. cylinder about 5 in. long and press in place at bottom edge of figure. Trim length if needed and smooth seam.

ELF: Repeat Santa's directions to make elf, using green for body and arms and red for hands.

Make red hat as directed for Santa, eliminating white band. Shape hat as shown in photo.

Roll out yellow to 1/8-in. thickness and cut out star. Add star to upright point of hat.

FINISHING: Bake figures according to manufacturer's directions. When cool, remove paper cones.

If desired, use a paintbrush to apply glaze to figures, following manufacturer's directions. 🌿

SANTA AND ELF PATTERNS

CONE PATTERN
Trace 1—tracing paper
Cut 2—brown paper
grocery sack

STAR PATTERN
Trace 1—tracing paper
Cut 1—yellow clay

Colorful Skirt Surrounds Tree Stylishly

MAKING the rounds will be an extra cheery affair when you crochet this well-toned tree skirt.

Not content to use a single set of stitches or just one color, Sue Childress of Longview, Texas switched stitch combinations and hues every few rows. "It's an interesting project to do, particularly if you've crocheted before," Sue reports.

Materials Needed:
Worsted-weight yarn in 3-1/2-ounce skeins with 246 yards/100 grams per skein—three skeins each of red, green and white
Size G/6 (4.25mm) crochet hook
Sue used Patons Canadiana Yarn in Cardinal, Old Christmas Green and White. If you use a different yarn, be sure to purchase the amount based on yardage per skein not ounces per skein.

Gauge: In dc, 4 sts and 2 rows = 1 inch.

Finished Size: Tree skirt measures about 48 inches across.

Special Stitches:
SHELL (SH): (2 dc, ch 2, 2 dc) in sp or st indicated.
V-STITCH (V-st): (Dc, ch 2, dc) in sp or st indicated.
DOUBLE CROCHET CLUSTER (dc Cl): Holding back last loop, 4 dc in stitch indicated, yo, draw through 5 loops on hk.
PICOT (picot): Ch 3, sc in third ch from hk.
FRONT POST and BACK POST STITCH (FP dc, BP dc): Work around post from back or front of stitch in dc.

Directions:
With red, ch 83.

Row 1: Hdc in third ch from hk and next 4 chs, [work 2 hdc in next ch, hdc in next 6 chs] across to last 6 chs, work 2 hdc in next ch, hdc in last 5 chs, turn.

Row 2: Ch 3, [sk 1 hdc, work 3 dc in next hdc] across to last hdc, sk last hdc, dc in top of beginning ch, turn: 45 sets of 3 dc.

Rows 3-6: Ch 3, work 3 dc in center dc of each 3-dc group, dc in top of turning ch-3, turn.

Row 7: Ch 3, work 4 dc in center dc of each 3-dc group across, dc in top of turning ch-3, fasten off, turn.

Row 8: Attach white in first dc, ch 3, [V-st in second dc of 4 dc-group, ch 2] across, dc in top of turning ch-3, turn: 45 V-sts.

Row 9: Ch 5, [V-st in next V-st, ch 2] across, dc in top of turning ch-3, turn.

Row 10: Ch 6, [V-st in next V-st, ch 3] across, dc in third ch of turning ch-5, fasten off, turn.

Row 11: Attach green in first dc, ch 4, [SH in V-st, ch 1] across, dc in third ch of turning ch-6, turn: 45 SHS.

Rows 12-13: Ch 5, [SH in SH, ch 2] across, dc in third ch of turning ch, turn.

Rows 14-15: Ch 6, [SH in SH, ch 3] across, dc in third ch of turning ch. At end of Row 15, fasten off, turn.

Row 16: Attach white in first dc, ch 5, [dc Cl in ch-3 sp, ch 3, dc Cl in SH sp, ch 3] across, dc in third ch of turning ch, turn: 90 dc Cl.

Rows 17-18: Ch 5, [dc Cl, ch 3] in each ch-3 sp across, ch 3, dc in third ch of turning ch, fasten off at end of Row 18, turn: 90 dc Cl.

Row 19: Attach red in first dc, ch 3, 2 dc in first ch-3 sp, [4 dc in next ch-3 sp, 3 dc in next ch-3 sp] across, ending with 4 dc in last ch-3 sp, 3 dc in ch-5 sp, turn: 318 dc counting the turning ch-3 as a dc.

Row 20: Ch 3, [skip next dc, dc in next dc, dc in skipped dc] across, dc in top of turning ch-3, turn.

Row 21: Ch 3, [dc in next 6 dc, work 2 dc in next dc] across, skip last dc, dc in top of turning ch-3, turn: 362 dc counting turning ch.

Row 22: Repeat Row 20.

Row 23: Ch 3, dc in next dc and each dc across, dc in top of turning ch, turn.

Row 24: Repeat Row 20, fasten off, turn.

Row 25: Attach white in last dc, ch 1, sc in next dc, [sk 1 dc, dc in 2 dc, work 3 dc in next dc, dc in next 2 dc, sk 1 dc, sc in next dc] across, ending with last sc in top of turning ch-3, turn.

Row 26: Ch 2, hdc in same sc, [dc in 3 dc, work 3 dc in next dc, dc in 3 dc, work 2 hdc in sc] across, fasten off, turn.

Row 27: Attach green in first hdc, [ch 5, sk 2 sts, sc in next st] across, turn: 165 ch-5 sps.

Row 28: Ch 3, work 4 dc in each ch-5 sp across, turn.

Row 29: [Ch 5, sc between next two 4-dc groups] across, ch 5, sc in last dc, turn.

Row 30: Repeat Row 28.

Row 31: Ch 3, dc in same dc and each dc across, dc in top of turning ch-3, fasten off, turn: 662 dc.

Row 32: Attach white in first dc, ch 3, [FP dc in next 2 dc, BP dc in next 2 dc] across, dc in top of turning ch-3, turn.

Row 33: Ch 3, [FP dc in FP dc, BP dc in BP dc] across, dc in top of turning ch-3, turn.

Row 34: Ch 3, dc in next dc and each dc across, fasten off, turn.

Row 35: Attach red in first dc, ch 1, sc in same st, [sk 2 dc, work 5 dc in next dc, sk 2 dc, sc in next dc] across, ending with last sc in top of turning ch-3, turn.

Row 36: Ch 1, sc in first sc, * (dc in next dc, make picot) 5 times across 5-dc group, sc in sc*. Repeat between *'s across. Do not turn, working in ends of rows, (work 3 sc around posts at end of rows) across to top edge; along original ch (sc in next 3 chs, sc next 2 chs together) across to other side, (work 3 sc around posts at end of rows) to beginning ch-1, end with slip stitch in beginning ch-1, fasten off.

ABBREVIATIONS	
ch(s)	chain(s)
dc(s)	double crochet(s)
hdc	half double crochet
hk	hook
lp(s)	loop(s)
sc	single crochet
sk	skip or skipped
sp(s)	space(s)
st(s)	stitches(s)
yo	yarn over
*, ( ) or [ ]	Instructions between asterisks, parentheses or brackets are repeated as indicated.

Brushes Shift Simple Blocks Into Gaily Wrapped Bundles

WHAT can be done with pieces of plain old wood? Plenty…in a country crafter's hands!

Pat Reid of Newcastle, Oklahoma applied bright "wrapping paper"—in the form of painted stripes, polka dots and clever holiday designs—to wood blocks she had handy, then stacked the "gift boxes" to create her trims.

"They're easy and fun," Pat sums up. "Plus, the colors can be changed to suit any decor."

Materials Needed (for both trims):
Pattern on this page
Tracing paper and pencil
Transfer paper
Paper plate or palette
Acrylic craft paints—blue, bright red, green, metallic gold and white for holly trim; bright red, flesh, green and white for Santa trim
Paintbrushes—Nos. 2 and 10 flat and liner
Band or scroll saw
Wood scraps—one 1-inch x 1-1/2-inch piece of 1/2-inch-thick, one 1-1/2-inch square of 3/4-inch-thick and one 1-1/2-inch x 2-1/2-inch piece of 3/4-inch-thick for holly trim; one 1-1/4-inch cube, one 1-1/2-inch x 2-1/2-inch piece of 3/8-inch-thick and
one 2-inch x 3-inch piece of 3/4-inch-thick for Santa trim
Wood sealer
Sandpaper
Tack cloth
Black fine-line permanent marker
Oak stain (optional)
Matte finish spray varnish
Wood glue
30 inches of 2-ply jute string for each
One gold 12mm jingle bell for each

Finished Size: Holly trim is 2-1/2 inches tall x 2-1/2 inches wide. Santa trim is 3 inches tall x 3 inches wide.

Directions:
Trace Santa pattern at right onto tracing paper.

Sand wood blocks and wipe with tack cloth to remove sanding dust. Apply wood sealer to all sides of wood blocks. Sand gently and wipe with tack cloth.

PAINTING: Referring to pattern, photo above and instructions below, paint blocks as follows:

Holly trim: Using larger flat brush, paint 1-in. x 1-1/2-in. rectangle blue and 1-1/2-in. square white. Paint blue, green and red stripes on 1-1/2-in. x 2-1/2-in. rectangle. Let dry.

Using No. 2 flat brush, paint white check design on blue block.

Using liner, paint green holly freehand on white block.

Use handle of brush to dab on red holly berries and red corner dots on white block. In same way, dab white dots on striped block. Using liner and gold, paint lines between stripes. Let dry.

Santa trim: Using larger flat brush, paint 1-1/4-in. cube and 2-in. x 3-in. rectangle green. Paint 1-1/2-in. x 2-1/2-in. rectangle red. Let dry.

Place transfer paper between pattern and 1-1/4-in. green cube and trace over Santa design.

Using No. 2 flat brush, paint Santa's face flesh, hat red and beard and fur trim white. Let dry.

Use handle of brush to dab on red dots for Santa's nose, mouth and cheeks. Let dry.

Using liner, paint mustache and eyebrows white. Let dry.

Use marker to add eyes and to outline eyebrows, mustache, face, fur trim, hat, pom-pom and beard.

Using No. 2 flat brush, paint green plaid design on red rectangle. When dry, use liner to paint white stripes on green plaid.

To paint snowflakes on the edges of green rectangle, use liner and white to paint lines as shown in Fig. 1. Then use handle of brush to dab a white dot in center of each snowflake and at the ends of each line.

FINISHING: Sand edges of wood pieces until wood shows. If desired, apply oak stain to edges for an aged look. Spray with sealer. Let dry.

Glue pieces together as shown in photo. Wrap jute around blocks. Thread jingle bell and tie in bow.

Fig. 1 Painting snowflakes

SANTA PATTERN
Trace 1—tracing paper
Paint as directed

Scenic Runner's Tops at Table Trimming

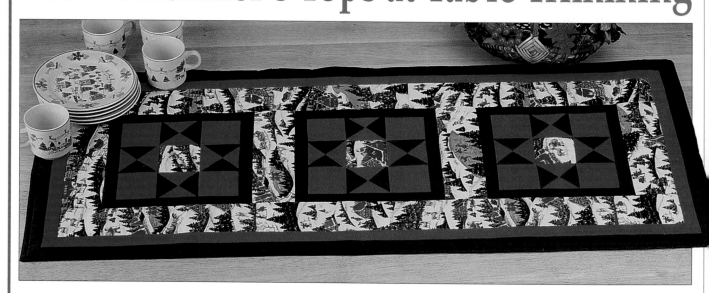

SERVING UP holiday spirit at mealtimes is the Christmasy chore this patchwork table runner will happily perform, time after time.

Its sturdy construction and scenic look are the work of crafter Jean Devore of Jackson, Missouri. "I relied on fabric with a fun wintry vista, but any kind of print will work," she divulges. "It's quite a conversation piece at our house."

Materials Needed:
44-inch-wide 100% cotton fabrics—
* 1-1/2 yards each of scenic or holiday print for center blocks and sashings, muslin for backing, red solid for blocks and borders and green solid for blocks, borders and binding*
50-inch x 25-inch piece of lightweight batting
Matching all-purpose thread
Monofilament thread
Rotary cutter and mat (optional)
Quilter's marking pen or pencil
Standard sewing supplies

Finished Size: Table runner measures 49-1/2 inches x 21-1/2 inches.

Directions:
Pre-wash, dry and press all fabrics.

Do all piecing with accurate 1/4-in. seams and right sides of fabrics together. Press seams toward darker fabrics when possible unless otherwise directed.

CUTTING: Accurately cut fabrics using rotary cutter and quilter's ruler or mark fabrics using ruler and marker of choice and cut with scissors. Cut lengthwise and crosswise strips as directed.

From scenic or holiday print, cut three 3-1/2-in. squares, taking care to center (fussy-cut) a scene in each if using a scenic print. Also cut two 3-1/2-in. x 48-in. pieces (cut lengthwise) and four 3-1/2-in. x 12-in. pieces (cut crosswise) for sashings, again taking care to center or fussy-cut scenes in each if using a scenic print.

From red solid, cut two 1-1/2-in. x 48-in. lengthwise strips for inside side borders and two 1-1/2-in. x 20-in. lengthwise strips for inside end borders. Cut one 3-1/4-in. x 44-in. strip for piecing. Also cut one 3-1/2-in. x 44-in. strip and from this strip cut twelve 3-1/2-in. squares for blocks.

From green solid, cut two 1-1/2-in. x 50-in. lengthwise strips for side borders and two 1-1/2-in. x 22-in. lengthwise strips for end borders. For borders around blocks, cut twelve 1-1/2-in. x 12-in. strips. Cut one 3-1/4-in. x 44-in. strip for piecing and three 2-1/2-in. x 54-in. strips for binding.

PIECING: Place a red and a green 3-1/4-in. x 44-in. strip right sides together with edges matching. Machine-stitch both long edges with a 1/4-in. seam. Cut a 3-1/4-in. square from strip. See Fig. 1.

Cut this square in half diagonally (see Fig. 2a). Open pieced triangles and press seams open. See Fig. 2b.

Pin long edges of green/red triangles right sides together, carefully matching seams. Sew long edges together. See Fig. 3a. Open to form a pieced square as shown in Fig. 3b. Press seam open.

With inside points of triangles centered, trim pieced square to an accurate 3-1/2-in. square. See Fig. 4.

Repeat piecing instructions, making a total of 12 green/red pieced squares.

BLOCK ASSEMBLY (make three): Lay out squares as shown in Assembly Diagram (Fig. 5). Sew together in rows, then sew rows together, forming a pieced block.

Sew one green border strip to top edge of pieced block and trim to fit. Stitch another border strip to bottom edge and trim to fit. Add side border strips in the same manner. Repeat, making a total of three blocks with green borders.

SASHING: Making sure all scenic or holiday prints are running in the same direction, sew a crosswise sashing piece between each block and at each end of the block strip as shown in photo above. Trim sashing even with the green side borders. In the same way, sew lengthwise sashing pieces to the sides of the block strip and trim even with the edges of the sashings at each end.

BORDERS: Stitch one 48-in. red border strip to one side edge of sashing and trim length to fit. Stitch a matching red border strip to opposite side edge of sashing and trim length to fit. Add remaining 20-in. strips to each end in the same way.

Stitch one 50-in. green border strip to one side edge of red border and trim length to fit. Stitch a matching green border strip to opposite side edge of red border and trim length to fit. Add remaining 22-in. strips to top and bottom edges in the same way.

QUILTING: Cut a 50-in. x 25-in. piece of muslin for backing. Place backing wrong side up on a flat surface and smooth out. Place batting over backing,

smoothing out wrinkles. Place pieced table runner on top of batting with right side up. Hand-baste layers together about every 4 in., avoiding seams.

Using monofilament thread on top and off-white thread in the bobbin, stitch-in-the-ditch of all pieced block and border seams, working from the center

out. Machine-baste around outer edges. Trim batting and backing even with pieced table runner.

BINDING: Stitch the short ends of the green binding strips together to make one long strip. Fold in half lengthwise with wrong sides together and press.

Pin binding to right side of table run-

ner, matching raw edges. Beginning with a 1/4-in. fold to the wrong side, stitch binding to table runner with a 1/4-in. seam, mitering corners. Overlap ends of binding and trim away excess. Turn and pin binding to wrong side, mitering corners and covering seam. Hand-stitch binding to backing, covering seam.

Fig. 1
Piecing strip

Cut 3-1/4-in. squares
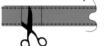
1/4-in. seams

Fig. 2a
Cut 3-1/4-in. square for two pieced triangles in half diagonally

Fig. 2b
Open pieced triangles and press

Fig. 5 Assembly Diagram

Fig. 3a
Stitch pieced triangles together

Fig. 3b
Pieced square

Fig. 4
Trim to 3-1/2-in. square

Delicious Decorating Starts With Dried-Apple Wreaths

RIPE for a down-home holiday trim, especially one you can work up in a jiffy? This appealing idea will suit your needs —and then some!

Made from dried apples, the mini-wreaths are a cinch to assemble, reveals Chris Korsmo, from Grand Marais, Michigan. "You just arrange slices and glue them together," she says.

"They look pretty hanging on the tree, in a window or from any spot that needs a touch of country."

Materials Needed (for one wreath):
Three dried Red Delicious apple slices*
Two small pinecones (about 1-1/4 inches each)
12 inches of 1/4-inch-wide red or green satin ribbon
Craft knife

White (tacky) glue
Clear acrylic spray sealer
Scissors
*To dry apple slices, remove core and cut apple across the core area into 1/4-inch-thick slices. Arrange slices in a single layer on wire rack and dry in a 175° oven for 7-8 hours. Or dry in food dehydrator following manufacturer's directions. When dry, apples will look somewhat shriveled but will still be pliable.

Finished Size: Apple wreaths measure approximately 3 inches across.

Directions:
Cut three dried apple slices in half. Arrange six half slices in a circle, with ends overlapping and apple peel on outside of circle as shown in photo above right. Glue slices together. Let dry.

Spray both sides of apple wreath with clear acrylic sealer, making sure to coat wreath thoroughly. Let dry.

FINISHING: Cut a 4-in. length of ribbon. Overlap cut ends and glue to front of apple wreath to form a loop as shown in photo. Tie remaining length of ribbon into a bow and glue bow over ends of ribbon loop. Trim ends of bow at an angle.

Glue two pinecones under bow as shown in photo.

With Church in the Window, Folks'll Like Seeing Double

FROM start to finish, you'll find it's an uplifting experience to brighten your rural view with this adornment that genuinely celebrates December 25.

The plastic canvas project is an easy one, assures designer Mary Cosgrove of Rockville, Connecticut. "The decoration is double-sided," she also points out, "which means it can be enjoyed both indoors and out hung in a window."

Materials Needed:

Chart on next page
Two pieces of 7-count plastic canvas, each 32 bars x 32 bars
Worsted-weight or plastic canvas yarn—10 yards each of white, Christmas red, yellow, bright blue, Christmas green and black*
1/3 yard of medium black braid*
Two 6-inch pieces of 1/8-inch-wide red metallic ribbon or yarn for bow*
4 yards of 1/8-inch-wide lemon-lime ribbon*
Small amount of polyester stuffing
Size 16 tapestry needle
Nylon thread
Scissors
*Mary used Needloft 2-ply plastic canvas yarn, Kreinik Hi-Lustre Black Medi-

um Braid and Kreinik Hi-Lustre 1/8-inch-wide Glow-In-The-Dark Lemon-Lime and Red ribbons.

Finished Size: Church window trim is about 5-1/4 inches high x 6-3/4 inches across.

Directions:

Being sure to count the bars and not the holes, cut two pieces of plastic canvas according to the chart.

Cut 18-in. lengths of yarn. Do not knot the yarn on back of work. Instead, leave a 1-in. tail on the back and catch it in the first few stitches. To end a yarn, run yarn on back of canvas under completed stitches of the same color and clip close to work.

Following the chart and referring to Fig. 1 for stitch illustrations, stitch each piece separately as follows: Work Continental stitches in red, white and yellow as indicated on chart.

Using green, cross-stitch wreath and straight-stitch trees.

Using black, backstitch around doors and straight-stitch steps. Using red, backstitch around windows.

Using black braid, backstitch cross on steeple over white.

Using blue, stitch center of border, leaving outside edges unstitched.

Using a 6-in. piece of red metallic ribbon or yarn, bring ends to front from back of canvas at bow placement "X" and tie a small bow.

FINISHING: Holding wrong sides of both completed pieces together and matching edges, whipstitch the inside edges of border with bright blue.

With lemon-lime ribbon and two stitches per hole, whipstitch outside edges of border and church, adding a small amount of stuffing between the layers of the church as you stitch.

To hang trim, loop a short length of nylon thread through top of border and knot ends together.

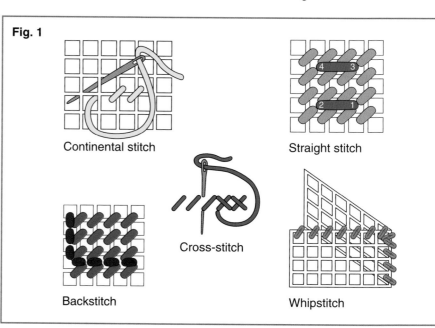

Fig. 1

Continental stitch

Straight stitch

Cross-stitch

Backstitch

Whipstitch

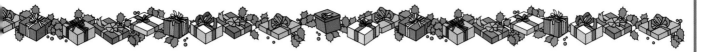

CHURCH WINDOW TRIM CHART
(Cut 2—32 bars x 32 bars—discard shaded portions)
X = bow placement

CHURCH WINDOW TRIM

COLOR KEY		Needloft			Needloft	Kreinik
⊘	White	41		**BACKSTITCH**		
◗	Christmas Red	02	◢	Black Braid		05HL
⊘	Yellow	57	◗	Black		00
◗	Bright Blue	60	⊘	Christmas Red		
CROSS-STITCH				(1 ply)		02
✚	Christmas Green	28		**WHIPSTITCH**		
STRAIGHT STITCH			▬	Bright Blue		60
▬	Black	00	═	Lemon-lime ribbon		054F
▬	Christmas Green	28		**BOW**—Red ribbon		003HL

Bow Wreath Relays the Season's Greetings

ROUNDING UP gift bows is about all that's required to make this wreath! Pat Hyde of Charlotte, North Carolina simply glued bows she had handy (plus more she purchased at a post-Christmas sale) onto a straw wreath.

"It's easy and pretty," she details. "You can hang it on a door or place it on a table as part of a centerpiece."

Materials Needed:
12-inch-wide plastic-wrapped straw wreath form
3-inch purchased gift bows in assorted colors—approximately 55*
4 yards of matching 1/4-inch-wide curling ribbon
Low-temperature glue gun and glue sticks
Straight pins
Monofilament thread (optional)
Scissors
*Pat used Mylar bows in blue, gold, green, red and silver with matching 1/4-inch-wide Mylar curling ribbon.

Finished Size: Wreath measures about 15 inches across.

Directions:
Cut a 1-yd. piece of curling ribbon or monofilament thread and knot ends together. Drape over wreath. Slip loop through knotted end for hanger and spot-glue in place.

Trim backing on bows to about 1 in.

square. Remove paper backing from bows to expose adhesive. Glue bows onto plastic-wrapped wreath form, starting with a row in the center of the wreath. Continue gluing bows onto wreath, alternating colors and placing

bows close together to cover form.

Cut curling ribbon into 6-in. lengths and pull across blade of scissors to curl. Using straight pins, attach one end of each ribbon between bows randomly around the wreath. ❧

Striped Set Is Youthfully Suited for Holiday Giving

COMFORT AND FUN are at the heart of this bright-as-can-be holiday gift idea, according to Gayla Cox. She set about knitting the hat and mittens for her young son to wear while he plays outdoors during the winter months.

"What's more, it'll work just as nicely for a girl," reveals the Guthrie, Oklahoma homemaker.

Materials Needed:
Scraps of worsted-weight yarn in eight different colors of choice
Knitting needles—size 5 double-pointed (set of four) or size needed to obtain correct gauge
Size 16 tapestry needle
Stitch marker and ruler
Scissors

Finished Size: For Stocking Cap—directions are for Child's size Medium. Changes for Adult size are in parentheses. Cap is about 44 (48) inches long.

For Mittens—directions are for Child's size Medium. Changes for Adult Woman's size 7 are in parentheses.

Gauge: When working in St st, 22 sts and 26 rows = 4 inches.

KNITTING REMINDERS:
Changing colors: To avoid holes when changing colors, always pick up new color yarn from beneath the dropped yarn.
Working in rounds: Cast on sts on dp needles. Place a marker at beginning of round, moving marker with each round worked. Being careful not to twist sts, join last st to first st by pulling up yarn firmly and making first st with fourth needle.

Stitches Used:
Stockinette stitch: St st
   Every round: K all sts.
K 2, p 2 ribbing: K 2, p 2 rib
   Every round: K 2, p 2 around.

Directions:
STOCKING CAP: With dp needles, cast on 92(100) sts and divide sts on three needles. Join to form a circle.

Work k 2, p 2 rib evenly for 4 in.

Work in St st evenly for next 6 in., changing colors as desired and making color bands no less than 1 in. wide and no more than 5 in. wide throughout.

Continue working in St st as established, decreasing 2 sts randomly in every sixth round until 30 sts remain. Then decrease 5 sts randomly in every round until 5 sts remain.

Using tapestry needle, run yarn through last 5 sts. Draw up sts tightly and secure.

Tassel: Cut two 12-in. pieces of yarn and lay them in your palm, along the length of your hand. Wrap another piece of yarn around the width of your hand about 50 times and cut yarn. Tie the 12-in. lengths of yarn tightly around the bundle of yarn in your palm. Slip the yarn off your hand and cut through the loops directly across from knot. Tie a matching yarn around the tassel about 1-1/2 in. from cut ends. Sew tassel to tip of stocking cap.

MITTENS (make two): With dp needles, cast on 32(36) sts and divide sts on three needles. Join to form a circle.

Cuff: Work k 2, p 2 rib evenly for 3 in.: 32(36) sts.

* K 2, p 2 tog; rep from * around for one round: 24(27) sts.

* K 2, p 1; rep from * around for three rounds: 24(27) sts.

Hand: * K 2, inc 1 st in next p st; rep from * around for one round: 32(36) sts.

Change color, work even in St st on 32(36) sts for 2(2-3/4) in.

Change color, k 1 one round.

Thumb hole: Make thumb hole by using a scrap of different colored yarn to k 5(7) sts. Slip the sts back onto the needle they just came from and continue knitting around for 1-3/4(2) in. on the 32(36) sts.

End of hand: Change color and k evenly for two(four) rounds: 32(36) sts.

Change color and k evenly for three (four) rounds: 32(36) sts.

Dec Rounds: Round 1: [K 4(5), k 2 tog] 5 times, k 2(1): 27(31) sts.

Round 2: [K 3(4), k 2 tog] 5 times; k 2(1): 22(26) sts.

Round 3: [K 2(3), k 2 tog] 5 times; k 2(1): 17(21) sts.

Round 4: [K 1(2), k 2 tog] 5 times; k 2(1): 12(16) sts.

Round 5: For Child size only, k 2 tog around: 6 sts. (For Adult size only: [K 1, k 2 tog] 5 times; k 1: 11 sts.)

Round 6: (For Adult size only: K 2 tog around: 6 sts.)

Using tapestry needle, run yarn through last 6 sts. Draw up sts tightly and secure.

Thumb: Being careful not to twist sts, remove contrasting yarn scrap and slip 5(7) loops below thumb opening to dp needle; with second dp needle, pick up 1 st at side of hole and 2(3) sts above thumb opening; with third dp needle, pick up last 2(3) loops above thumb opening and 1 st at side of hole. Attach matching mitten yarn and knit one round in St st: 11(15) sts.

Thumb dec: Dec 1, then work around on 10(14) sts until thumb measures 1-3/4(2) in.

Change to color of narrow stripe on hand of mitten, k 3 rounds: 10(14) sts.

K 2 tog around: 5(7) sts.

Using tapestry needle, run yarn through last 5(7) sts. Draw up sts tightly and secure. Weave in loose ends on inside of mitten. Turn down cuff. Refold second mitten so the thumb is on the opposite side.

ABBREVIATIONS	
dec	decrease
dp	double-pointed
inc	increase
k	knit
p	purl
rep	repeat
st(s)	stitch(es)
tog	together
* or [ ]	Instructions following asterisk or between brackets are repeated as directed

Wintry Sock Dolls Are a Stocking Feat!

FEET FIRST is the approach Amy Albert Bloom of Shillington, Pennsylvania took with her outdoorsy dolls. To create them, she turned to children's cotton socks.

"These dolls make fun stocking stuffers," Amy notes, "or they can be hung from sturdy branches on the Christmas tree."

Materials Needed (for both dolls):
Pattern on this page
Tracing paper and pencil
Children's socks, size 4 to 6-1/2—one sock each in bright blue and yellow or two socks in colors of choice*
Matching all-purpose thread
Polyester stuffing
1-inch pom-poms—one each red and white
24 inches of string
Two 12-inch pieces of 1/16-inch-wide white ribbon for hangers (optional)
Three Popsicle or craft sticks
Scraps of felt—black, bright green, flesh, pink, red and yellow
1-inch x 12-inch pieces of felt—one each bright green and red
2 yards of gold yarn
Black fine-line permanent marker
Scrap of corrugated cardboard
Scrap of aluminum foil
Glue gun and glue sticks
Hand-sewing needle
Compass (optional)
Scissors

*Four dolls can be made from two pairs of children's socks.

Finished Size: Sock dolls are about 6-1/4 inches tall.

Directions:
Trace mitten pattern onto tracing paper and cut out. Cut felt mittens as directed. Use a compass to draw 1-1/2-in., 3/8-in. and 1/4-in. circle patterns onto tracing paper and cut out. Or cut circles out freehand.

BODY: Cut off foot of each sock at cuff. Set cuffs aside for stocking caps. Stuff the foot portions firmly to make a rounded body. Tuck in the raw edges and stitch around openings with a running stitch. See Fig. 1. Draw up thread to close opening. Knot threads and clip. This stitching will be at the back of the dolls.

Tie a piece of string around each sock about 2 in. from the toe to form neck. Knot string and clip close to neck.

For each doll, trace around circle patterns and cut one 1-1/2-in. flesh felt circle for face, two 1/4-in. black felt circles for eyes and two 3/8-in. pink felt circles for cheeks. Glue these to the front of each doll just above the neck as shown in photo below. Using black marker, draw a mouth on the face of each as shown in photo.

For stocking caps, sew around cut end of each cuff with running stitch. Draw up thread to close opening. Knot threads and clip. Fold 3/4 in. of cuff edge

up twice and hand-stitch or spot-glue to secure.

FINISHING: Skier Doll: Cut gold yarn into three equal lengths and knot together at one end. Braid yarn and knot end. Trim ends even. With knotted ends hanging down, glue braid centered across top of head of yellow doll. Glue bright blue stocking cap to top of head and white pom-pom to top of cap.

For scarf, cut a 1-in. x 12-in. piece of red felt. Make 1/2-in.-long cuts into both ends for fringe as shown in photo. Tie scarf around doll's neck.

Cut two 1/2-in. x 2-in. pieces of red felt and glue around Popsicle or craft sticks for ski bindings as shown in photo. Glue skis to doll's body and green mittens over skis.

If desired, stitch white ribbon through top of stocking cap and tie ends in overhand knot for hanger. Trim ends of ribbon to desired length.

Snow Shovel Doll: Glue yellow stocking cap on top of head of blue doll and red pom-pom on top of cap.

Make scarf from green felt as directed above and tie around doll's neck.

Cut a 1-1/2-in. x 2-in. piece of corrugated cardboard. Roll cardboard slightly to create a curved shovel shape and cover with aluminum foil. Glue Popsicle or craft stick to foil-covered cardboard as shown in photo. Glue shovel to doll's body and yellow mittens over shovel handle. Attach hanger as directed above if desired.

SOCK DOLLS MITTEN PATTERN
Trace 1—tracing paper
Cut 2 each—doubled bright green and red felt

Fig. 1 Running stitch

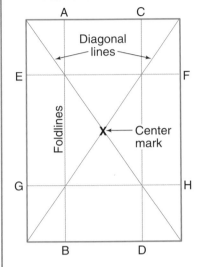

Fig. 1
Mark and fold card

Fig. 2
Cut along A-B and C-D foldlines as shown

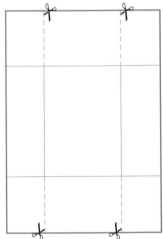

Fig. 3
Form box

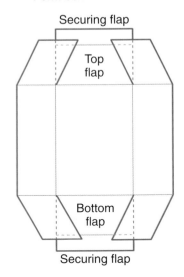

Christmas Cards Carry on As Fast-to-Form Gift Boxes

DON'T DISCARD the cards you receive at Christmas! Sharon Egger of Hickman, Nebraska shares how she turns her treasured greetings into pretty little gift boxes.

Children can fold these up in a flash, using just a ruler, pencil and a bit of glue. Plus, the boxes will save time and money in another way—they need no gift wrap.

Materials Needed (for one):
Christmas card
Scissors or rotary cutter and mat
Ruler
Pencil
Eraser
Tacky (white) glue

Finished Size: The size of the card box will vary depending on the size of the card used.

Directions:
Cut card along fold in order to form front and back sections. The front of the card will form the top of the box, and the back will form the bottom.

Cut off a scant 1/8 in. on two adjoining sides of back section so bottom of box will be slightly smaller than the top.

Mark the center on the inside of the front and back sections by lightly drawing a pencil line diagonally from corner to corner. Repeat with remaining corners to form an "X".

Referring to Fig. 1, fold both side edges of back section to center mark and crease sharply, making foldlines A-B and C-D. Unfold. In the same way, fold top and bottom edges to center mark, making foldlines E-F and G-H. Cut to folds on A-B and C-D crease lines as shown in Fig. 2. Erase pencil lines.

Fold up sides and bring corners in toward center. Fold the top and bottom flaps up and the securing flaps over corners as shown in Fig. 3. Glue the securing flaps in place. If your card is square, the securing flaps will be omitted. Repeat with front section of card to form top of box.

Place top over bottom to complete gift box.

There Is More Than Meets The Eye to This Ornament!

FASHIONING FUN—in more ways than one—is the assignment this appealing attire from Bette Veinot of Bridgewater, Nova Scotia happily fulfills. Not only are her Santa's britches easy on the eyes, they'll enhance the room with a pleasing aroma—thanks to the potpourri you tuck inside—when you hang them on the tree.

Materials Needed:

Pattern on this page
Tracing paper and pencil
Scrap or one 5-1/4-inch x 8-1/2-inch piece of striped Christmas print or fabric of choice
1/2 yard of 1/4-inch-wide red satin picot ribbon or color of choice
Two 3/8-inch red buttons or color of choice
Glue gun and glue sticks
Matching all-purpose thread
Standard sewing supplies
Potpourri

Finished Size: Britches are 3-1/2 inches across x 6 inches tall, including suspenders.

Directions:

Trace pattern at right onto tracing paper and cut fabric as directed. Fold fabric in half with right sides together, making a 4-1/4-in. x 5-1/4-in. rectangle. Stitch the 5-1/4-in. edges together with a 1/4-in. seam.

Mark stitching lines for leg seam as shown on pattern. Stitch leg seam through both layers of fabric, backstitching at beginning and end of seam and leaving needle in fabric while turning at point. Trim seam to 1/8 in. and clip to point.

Fold down other edge 1/2 in. to wrong side to form a hem. Hand-stitch 1/4 in. from fold, using a running stitch (see Fig. 1). Stitch another row 1/8 in. below first row and draw up stitches until waist measures about 1-3/4 in. across. Knot and clip threads.

Make leg hems in the same manner, drawing up stitches until leg openings measure about 3/4 in. across.

Turn britches inside out. Place a small amount of glue at leg gathers to keep potpourri inside.

FINISHING: Cut two 5-in. pieces of ribbon and stitch the ends of each together to make two loops for suspenders. Hand-stitch each suspender to inside of waist as shown in photo at right.

Insert potpourri through waist opening.

Sew buttons onto front as shown in photo, stitching through ribbon suspenders and waist of britches.

Cut remaining ribbon in half and make two bows. Glue a bow to each leg above gathers as shown in photo. Trim ends of ribbon at an angle.

Fig. 1 Running stitch

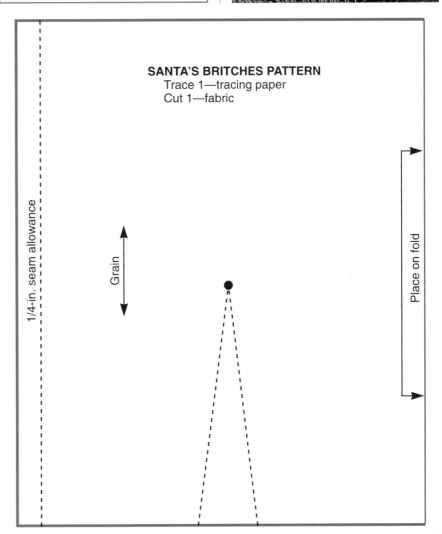

SANTA'S BRITCHES PATTERN
Trace 1—tracing paper
Cut 1—fabric

1/4-in. seam allowance

Grain

Place on fold

Spicy Yule Stitches Produce Treats Good Enough to Eat

NO, it's not edible. Still, you can count on folks enjoying this variation of a traditional Christmas treat.

To create it, Penny Duff of Kennebunk, Maine translated gingerbread cutouts into cross-stitch, using the colors of the season. Her eye-appealing picture will brighten your home wherever you hang it.

Materials Needed:
Chart on this page
9-inch x 12-inch piece of white 14-count Aida cloth
DMC six-strand embroidery floss in colors listed on color key
Size 24 tapestry needle
Scissors
Picture frame

Finished Size: Gingerbread design is 4-1/2 inches x 7-1/2 inches. Design area is 57 stitches x 101 stitches.

Directions:
Zigzag or overcast edges of Aida cloth to prevent fraying. Fold cloth in half lengthwise, then fold in half crosswise to determine center and mark this point. To find center of chart, draw lines across chart connecting arrows. Begin stitching at this point so design will be centered.

Working with 18-inch lengths of six-strand floss, separate strands and use three strands for cross-stitching and one

GINGERBREAD PICTURE CHART

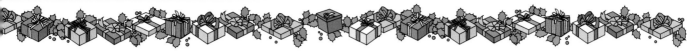

strand for backstitching. See Fig. 1 for stitch illustrations.

Each square on chart equals one stitch worked over a set of fabric threads. Use colors indicated on color key to complete cross-stitching first, then backstitching.

Do not knot floss on back of work. Instead, leave a short tail of floss on back of work and hold it in place while working the first few stitches around it. To end a strand, run needle under a few neighboring stitches in back before cutting floss close to work.

Frame as desired.

GINGERBREAD COLOR KEY

COLOR KEY		DMC
w	White	000
◪	Red	304
◲	Green	367
⊡	Dark Gold-Brown	420
⊡	Gold-Brown	422
◉	Very Dark Brown	801
△	Pink	899
⊠	Gold	3046

BACKSTITCHING
—	Dark Gold-Brown	420
—	Very Dark Brown	801

Fig. 1

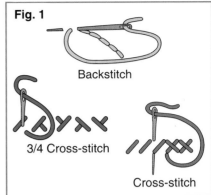

Backstitch

3/4 Cross-stitch

Cross-stitch

Angels Give Evergreens a Spirited Touch

CROCHET a whole host of these heavenly figures from Nancy Rhodes of Lake Pleasant, New York…and watch your tree take on a meaningful glow.

"I call them 'thumbnail angels' because they're so small," reveals Nancy. "Each is crocheted in one piece and takes less than an hour from start to finish."

Materials Needed (for one angel):
One ball of size 10 crochet cotton— white or ecru
Size 1 (3.00mm) steel crochet hook
Cotton ball or polyester stuffing for head
6 inches of 1/8-inch-wide satin ribbon in color of choice (optional)
One 1/4-inch-diameter ribbon rose in color of choice (optional)
6 inches of metallic cord for hanger
Small safety pin or contrasting thread

Finished Size: Each crocheted angel is about 2-3/4 inches tall x 1-1/2 inches across.

Gauge: 7 sc = 1 inch.

Special Stitches:
SINGLE CROCHET DECREASE (sc dec): Draw up a lp in each of next two sts, yarn over and draw through all lps on hk. One sc dec made.
V-STITCH SHELL (V-st Sh): Work dc, ch 1, dc in same stitch or space as directed.

Directions:
Notes: Head is worked in continuous rounds; do not join. Mark rounds with safety pin or thread. Work picots tightly to help make the wings stand up.

HEAD: Round 1: Ch 3, work 7 sc in third ch from hk.

Round 2: Work 2 sc in each st: 14 sc.

Rounds 3-4: Sc in each st around: 14 sc.

Round 5: * Sc in next 2 sts, work 1 sc dec over next 2 sc; repeat from * around until 8 sts remain.

Stuff head with cotton ball or polyester stuffing.

WINGS AND BODICE: Round 6: Sl st in next st, ch 4, dc in same st (counts as first V-st Sh), work 1 V-st Sh in each st around. Join with sl st in third ch of beginning ch-4: 8 V-st Shs.

Round 7: Sl st to first ch-sp, * work 3 dc in ch-sp, ch 3, sl st in third ch from hk (picot made), work 3 dc in same sp; sc in sp between V-st Shs *; repeat between *'s two more times; work 3 scs across next V-st Sh. Repeat between *'s three times, work 3 scs across next V-st Sh .

DRESS: Round 8: Holding all other stitches out of the way and working across the two sets of scs only, ch 4, dc in first sc (counts as first V-st Sh), work 1 V-st Sh in each sc around. Join with sl st in ch 3 of beginning ch: 6 V-st Shs.

Round 9: Sl st to first ch-1 sp of V-st Sh, ch 4, dc in same st (counts as first V-st Sh); work 1 V-st Sh in each ch-1 sp and between each V-st Sh: 12 V-st Shs.

Rounds 10-12: Work 1 V-st Sh in each V-st Sh around: 12 V-st Shs.

Rounds 13-14: Sc in each st around. Sl st in next st and fasten off.

FINISHING: Stitch a ribbon rose and/or a small bow to angel's bodice as shown in photo below.

Tie gold cord in overhand knot and stitch to back of head for hanger.

ABBREVIATIONS
ch	chain
dc	double crochet
dec	decrease
hk	hook
lp(s)	loop(s)
sc	single crochet
sl st	slip stitch
sp	space
st(s)	stitch(es)

Felt Scene Affirms Season's Reason

THIS JOYOUS ENSEMBLE makes a most meaningful addition to holiday decorating. Farm wife Janna Britton of Firebaugh, California used felt to assemble her figures. "They're touchable and colorful," she says, "perfect for a country setting."

Materials Needed:
Patterns on next page
Tracing paper and pencil
Felt scraps—black, brown, cinnamon, cream, gray-blue, gray heather, light blue, red and white
2-inch x 3-inch scrap of green and tan striped fabric for Joseph's robe
9 inches of lightweight nylon cord or heavy crochet cotton
Four 3-3/4-inch clothespins (also called doll pins) with matching doll pin stands
Band or scroll saw
Toothpick
Fabric paints—black and brown
Glue gun and glue sticks
Hand-sewing needle and blue thread
Scissors

Finished Size: Joseph is about 5-1/4 inches tall x 2-1/4 inches across. Mary is about 4-1/2 inches tall x 1-1/2 inches

across. Baby Jesus is about 2-1/2 inches long. The donkey is about 4-3/4 inches high x 4-3/4 inches across.

Directions:
Fold tracing paper in half. With fold of paper matching foldline of patterns, trace Mary's hair, cloak, dress, arms and body, Joseph's body, cloak and hair and the blanket onto tracing paper. Cut out and unfold for complete patterns. On unfolded tracing paper, trace the remaining patterns and cut out.

Cut out felt pieces as directed on patterns. Also cut one 1/4-in. x 1-1/2-in. piece of brown felt for Baby Jesus' hair.

Using scroll or band saw, cut 1 in. from prong ends of two doll pins for donkey's legs. Glue the prong ends of all four doll pins into the doll stands.

JOSEPH: Glue Joseph's striped robe fabric over body piece, matching bottom and side edges. Glue hair along curved top edge of body piece. Glue cloak front over robe and body pieces, matching outside edges. Glue beard to front of robe, leaving about 3/4 in. of face showing. Glue cloak back to cloak front along outside edges, leaving center of bottom edge open for doll pin. Trim outside edges as needed. Insert doll pin in bottom opening. Glue to secure.

MARY: Glue Mary's dress over body piece, matching bottom and side edges. Glue hair around face as shown in photo at left. Fold arms in half lengthwise and glue ends to outside edges of Mary's dress where indicated on pattern.

Using running stitch (see Fig. 1) about 1/8 in. from outside edge, gather the top edge of Mary's cloak. Glue top edge of cloak over hair. Wrap and glue sides of cloak over sides of Mary's dress as shown in photo. Insert doll pin in the bottom opening. Glue as needed to secure.

BABY JESUS: Glue felt hair piece around curved edge of Baby Jesus' body. Place Baby Jesus on blanket. Wrap and glue blanket around body, leaving about 1/2 in. of the face showing as shown in photo. Place Baby Jesus in Mary's arms and spot-glue to hold.

DONKEY: Fold ear as shown in photo. Glue mane and ear to wrong side of one donkey piece where shown on pattern. Place two donkey pieces wrong sides together and glue edges, encasing mane and ear and leaving opening for doll pin legs as shown on pattern. Slip donkey over doll pins and glue in place. Knot ends of nylon cord or crochet cotton and spot-glue to donkey's head for reins as shown in photo.

FINISHING: Using toothpick dipped in brown paint, dab eyes on Joseph, Mary and Baby Jesus. In the same way, draw nose and mouth on each. Use toothpick dipped in black paint to dab eyes on each side of donkey's head where indicated on pattern. ❦

Fig. 1   Running stitch

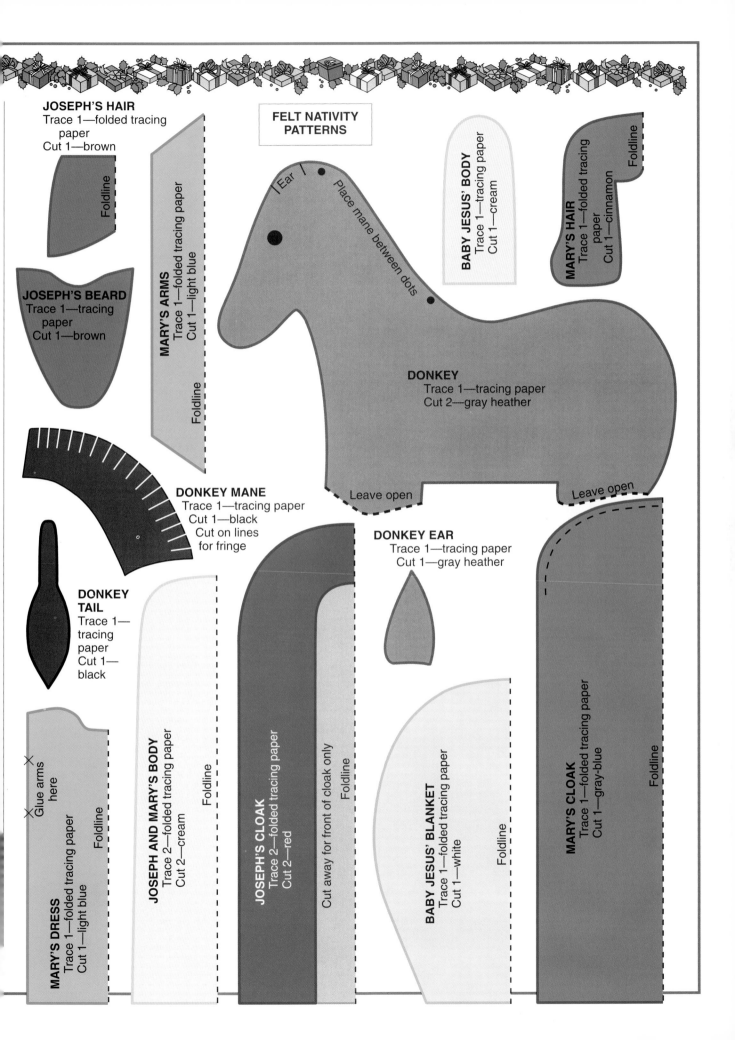

JOSEPH'S HAIR
Trace 1—folded tracing paper
Cut 1—brown

Foldline

FELT NATIVITY PATTERNS

BABY JESUS' BODY
Trace 1—tracing paper
Cut 1—cream

MARY'S HAIR
Trace 1—folded tracing paper
Cut 1—cinnamon

Foldline

JOSEPH'S BEARD
Trace 1—tracing paper
Cut 1—brown

MARY'S ARMS
Trace 1—folded tracing paper
Cut 1—light blue

Foldline

Ear

Place mane between dots

DONKEY
Trace 1—tracing paper
Cut 2—gray heather

Leave open

Leave open

DONKEY MANE
Trace 1—tracing paper
Cut 1—black
Cut on lines for fringe

DONKEY EAR
Trace 1—tracing paper
Cut 1—gray heather

DONKEY TAIL
Trace 1—tracing paper
Cut 1—black

Glue arms here

MARY'S DRESS
Trace 1—folded tracing paper
Cut 1—light blue

Foldline

JOSEPH AND MARY'S BODY
Trace 2—folded tracing paper
Cut 2—cream

Foldline

JOSEPH'S CLOAK
Trace 2—folded tracing paper
Cut 2—red

Cut away for front of cloak only

Foldline

BABY JESUS' BLANKET
Trace 1—folded tracing paper
Cut 1—white

Foldline

MARY'S CLOAK
Trace 1—folded tracing paper
Cut 1—gray-blue

Foldline

Unique Ornaments She Turns Out Are Also *from* the Tree

SURROUNDED by wood in her log house near Spring Green, Wisconsin, country crafter Kim Russell has carved out a comforting Christmas specialty that can't be duplicated—even by her.

"Every day in our workshop is like a holiday for my husband, Rob, and me," she beams. "I'm a real Christmas lover, and my particular niche is creating ornaments that celebrate the season."

Like dainty lace snowflakes, no two of Kim's delicately hand-hewn ornaments look exactly alike. Inspired by similar Victorian-era woodcrafts, she spent years perfecting the original patterns that add a beautiful new dimension to her Yuletide decor.

"I begin one of my 3-D snowflakes by attaching my pattern to birch plywood," she outlines. "Then I drill and cut out one design inside another with my scroll saw. Next, I separate the two pieces and dye them in Christmas colors—such as red, green and winter blue.

"To get the three-dimensional effect, I string them so the inner piece can be turned 90° and pressed flat again. That way, the snowflake can twirl gently on the tree and fold up for storage or for mailing in a Christmas card.

"I've also come up with wild birds, an angel and a twinkling star. I carve a large star as well—in three intricate pieces—to make a novel tree topper."

The roots of her artistry can be traced back to Kim's own family tree. "Traditionally, my brother, sisters and I trimmed our own tiny pine with ornaments we hand-fashioned," she recounts. "Now, our daughter, Neara, 10, helps Rob and me assemble ornaments—and does her own wooden cutouts in addition."

The result of all the ornament activity meets with a welcome reaction from those eager to recapture the true, tranquil nature of the Noel.

"People seem to appreciate the natural, old-fashioned feeling our wooden ornaments have," Kim reports. "They say that—instead of glitter and glass, flashing light bulbs and baubles—these simple silhouettes have a timelessness …one that takes them back to Christmases past."

Editor's Note: *Kim would be happy to send you a brochure about her hand-cut wood ornaments. To request one, write to Russellworks, E5502 Jones Rd., Spring Green WI 53588 or call her at 1-608/588-2765.*

HOLIDAY HEW. Kim Russell's in-home woodcraft business goes with the grain of her family. With help of daughter Neara (below), Kim coaxes forest-fresh snowflakes, birds out of birch trees.

For Tree-Grower Farm Wife, Fir Things Are Always First

ASK Ellen Church about her favorite holiday symbol and she won't skirt the issue. "Santa wouldn't have anyplace to put presents," she winks, "if it weren't for the Christmas tree!"

Thanks to the efforts of Ellen and her husband, Cline, St. Nick needn't concern himself with a shortage in that area. "Fraser firs thrive in our cool North Carolina mountains," Ellen observes from the 300-acre evergreen nursery she and Cline run outside Fleetwood.

"Growing our firs—plus white pine, Norway spruce and Canadian hemlock—cultivates our patience," she adds. "By the time they reach Christmas tree size, they're 12 years old."

The trees keep Christmas constantly on Ellen's mind.

"In spring, it's time for planting, fertilizing and weeding," she relates. "Come summer, we're pruning and shearing. Trees are harvested late October into December."

While the Churches' firs crop up in garden centers and commercial tree lots from Connecticut to Texas, part of the prickly inventory stays in an on-farm choose-and-cut plot for families pining for an old-fashioned experience.

Advises Ellen, "We find it so satisfying when families think enough of our greenery to keep returning. The annual growth of a tree is around 8 to 12 inches. Watching our customers' children change year to year, it seems they're sprouting up almost as fast!"

How about when it comes to choosing a Yule centerpiece for their own home? These evergreen-thumbed growers have become accustomed to pretty lofty expectations.

"Our daughter, Amber, 12, and son, Alex, 10, don't stop hunting until they find a tree that's at least 9 feet tall," Ellen chuckles.

But that's all right with this rural-rooted Santa's helper. "When we're decorating it," she reports, "we have a lot we like to think about—the thousands of other people gathered together around *our* family trees."

Editor's Note: *Ellen and Cline's choose-and-cut Christmas tree farm is open from the Friday after Thanksgiving through December 20. Hours are 10 a.m. to dusk. For more information or a price list, send a self-addressed stamped envelope to Cline Church Nursery, 10787 Hwy. 221 S, Fleetwood NC 28626. Or phone 1-910/877-4237.*

A CUTTING EDGE artisan, Kim logs plenty of hours fashioning filigree hearts and starburst tree toppers in busy backyard workshop.

JOLLY CROP gives Ellen Church (above) cause for celebrating Christmas all year long. Summer days find her pruning, shearing trees into "star material". Near Yuletide, children Amber, Alex tie up nursery's showpiece tree with ribbons.

IMPRESSIONS OF NOEL (above, below) are glowing examples of Sandra Siens Wallin's talent. Meddling with tin (left), she trims branches with magic of Christmas.

Metalsmith's Tin Tabulation Amounts to Merry Yuletide

REPEATING patterns from Christmas past, Sandra Siens Wallin of rural Vevay, Indiana forges right ahead.

"My husband, Jerry, and I are restoration metalsmiths," she says of their family business, Wallin Forge. "After learning the basics from him, I began re-creating tinware that reflects an earlier era."

Sandra's at-home tin shop makes it plain that Christmas proves her creative mettle. Delicate tin icicles drip from display boards along with hammered animal-shaped hangings. One work table's blanketed with brilliant star ornaments, while burnished hearts and cookie cutters fill another.

"German artisans, who invented tinplate, also originated the first decorated Christmas trees," she reveals. "For authenticity, I base my tin trimmings and other items on genuine pieces I find in metal collections and museums."

In turn, she notes, some of her reproductions end up in museums. "Besides Christmas decorations," Sandra adds, "I make pierced tin lanterns, chandeliers, wall sconces and candle holders. Once in a while, I even supply pioneer-style kitchen utensils as movie props."

Using old-fashioned tin shears, seamers, rollers and soldering tools, Sandra preserves an artistic tradition. "In many ways," she states, "tinsmithing is like making a dress. But instead of a pattern, you use a template.

"To make a Christmas star, I mark the template outline onto metal with an awl and then cut out the design with tinsnips. Next, I pound the edges smooth, rub with steel wool, and impress a pattern with a metal punch and mallet."

Abrim with Christmas spirit, Sandra doesn't let the busy tin business foil her home decorating plans. "Handmade tin pieces look lovely hanging on our evergreen and grapevine wreaths," she observes. "They also serve to brighten the garlands and swags I string across our soffit and fireplace mantel."

Shining equally bright for her is the knowledge her tin tends to tinker with customers' untarnished memories. "Seeing even a simple icicle brings back happy images to grandparents," Sandra smiles, "who then start to share Yuletide stories from their own childhood."

Editor's Note: *For more information on Sandra's historic tinware, send a self-addressed stamped envelope to Wallin Forge, 107 W. Market St., Vevay, IN 47043.*

A Doll for Christmas? She Does Santa Several Better!

LOTS OF women get dolled up for Christmas. Audrey McCully just does it a bit more playfully.

"My husband, Bill, and I don't have children at home any longer," relates the retiree from rural Prescott, Ontario. "But we're surrounded by wee people all the same. I have *200* dolls. And I get the whole 'family' together at Christmas."

Indeed, it's one dollightful greeting guests receive at the McCullys'. Dimpled baby dolls model red velvet dresses, and jolly Santas sport hand-crocheted vests. Flirtatious fashion dolls show off taffeta skirts, and cuddly cloth dolls wear green-ribboned tresses.

"I begin dressing my dolls for the holidays in late October and position them in every nook and cranny," Audrey relates. "Friends say those gathered by the fireplace look so realistic they half expect them to start singing carols."

The little characters made a big first impression on Audrey when her now-adult granddaughters were youngsters.

"The girls kept several of their dolls at our house, and over the years, 'Gram' sort of adopted them," she chuckles. "Soon, I was finding more at flea markets and thrift stores. In the meantime, friends were bringing me some of their children's outgrown favorites besides."

Today, it's small wonder Audrey "grandmothers" a clan that walks, talks, crawls, kisses and giggles. Her fanciful figures are made of vinyl, celluloid, porcelain and bisque.

"Since I've always enjoyed sewing," she adds, "I make all my dolls' outfits—often altering cast-off child-sized clothing.

"I've noticed my dolls bring out the excited child in everyone—more so than ever at Christmas. Kids of *all* ages visit and come back with their families."

This grandma knows, too, that a child can hardly resist squeezing her charming darlings. "So I've set aside my sturdiest and most huggable ones as official playmates," she reports. "After all, that's a doll's main purpose."

As for a husband whose wife toys with a pastime, "Bill takes it all in stride," she confides. "Not only does he smile when I bring home 'just one more' doll, he's built shelves to display them."

That's especially important this Christmas with one awestruck set of eyes. "Because of my hobby, I live in the biggest dollhouse little Baily has ever seen," Audrey beams about a real living doll…her new great-granddaughter!

"HAPPY DOLLY DAYS!" would be fitting Yule greeting for Audrey McCully to offer. Fun-loving collector (below) decks halls—and every room—with dolls she outfits in imaginative holiday styles.

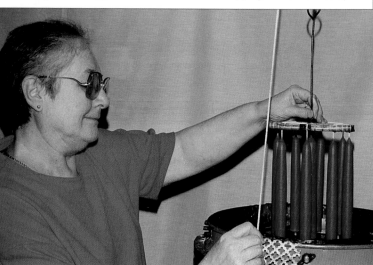

FESTIVE FLICKERS begin in hives Helen Riddle (above) and husband harvest. She then pours energy into handmade candles dripping with Christmas spirit.

It's Honey of a Holiday for Candle-Making Beekeeper

AT Helen Riddle's rural acres, it's beeginning to look a lot like Christmas. Waxing nostalgic—by crafting beeswax candles—is a bright holiday custom for the St. Marys, Pennsylvania farm wife.

"Honey's our principal product," she points out. "My husband, Marvin, and I keep 300 hives of bees. So I have *millions* of 'elves' helping to furnish the raw material for my dipped, rolled and molded candles."

That help's appreciated when her at-home shop starts storing tall tapers in rainbow colors that dangle from drying racks and chubby Santa candles that drip waxy whiskers.

"Hand-dipping the cotton wicks is work," she assures. "It takes 35 dips in-

to a vat of melted wax to make one 7/8-inch-diameter candle.

"I use beeswax sheets with a hexagonal pattern to fashion my rolled candles. They end up looking much like a real honeycomb does.

"Most of my candles have a Christmasy cast at present," she adds, happily opening molds to pop out poinsettias, evergreens and Nativities. "Beeswax has a high melting point. That means these candles could last season after festive season."

Helen's candle season gets under way half a year before the holidays arrive. "From June through September, Marvin and I extract honey from the comb by uncapping the wax pantries the bees

make," she says. "I take those caps, drain the excess honey, and melt and strain them to produce wax."

The candles that wax goes to form get decoratively around.

"Besides setting the tone for candle-light dinners," Helen notes, "they make cheerful displays and centerpieces. My Crown Candle design looks like a wax sculpture with its crisscrossing wicks and tapers. When all 18 candles are lit, it's a dazzling sight.

"I discovered candle crafts when I served as a leader for our children's 4-H club," Helen shares. "And I'm glad I did.

"As a farmer's daughter, I naturally grew up with 'waste not, want not' as my motto. So I'm excited about being able to use *every* item that our industrious honeybees produce!"

Editor's Note: *To receive details on ordering her beeswax candles, send a self-addressed stamped envelope to Helen Riddle, 1796 Bucktail Tr., St. Marys PA 15857 or telephone 1-814/834-3064.*

Christmas Past

I remember a long-ago Christmas
And the candles that lit up the tree;
Strung with popcorn and cranberry garlands,
It was dressed up so elegantly.

We would gather around the piano,
Singing carols with faces aglow;
Then we would steal away for a moment
With our beaus 'neath the mistletoe.

In the twilight we'd hitch up the horses
For a sleigh ride on snow-covered ground;
Soon harness bells jingling merrily
Filled the air with a holiday sound.

Christmas Day we would gather together
At the tiny white church on the hill
To honor the birth of the Savior—
In my mind, I envision it still.

Then surrounded by all of our loved ones,
We would open the gifts we received—
Simple presents tied up with bright ribbon…
But worth riches, everybody believed.

Though my heart may be filled with nostalgia,
Like a child I look forward with glee
To the holiday season that's coming…
And the magic of Christmas-to-be!

—Ruth Fiori Poynor
Boise, Idaho

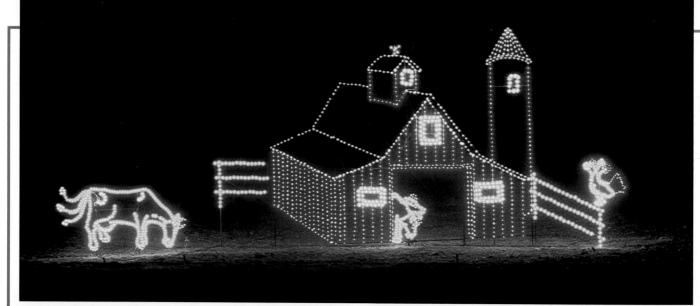

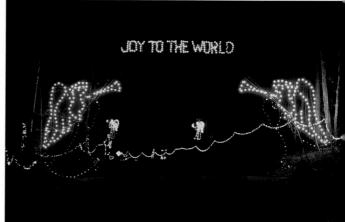

Farm Family Helps Folks See the Bright Side

FOR A SWITCH at Christmas, Kathy Burt forgets about crops—and charges ahead with putting her family's operation in a whole new light.

"Our 70-acre Appalachian Lights display is our effort to show the real meaning of this wondrous season," Kathy explains from the foothills farm-turned-Christmas card she runs with her husband, Johnny, near Dawsonville, Georgia. "This time of year, it's holiday spirits we raise rather than pumpkins, gourds, squash and corn.

"Our display uses over half a million lights in some 40 different scenes featuring rural, fantasy and religious Christmas themes," she details.

"To take it all in, you can drive the 2-mile route yourself. Or you can climb aboard our covered wagon. We have a team of green 'Deeres' to pull it!

"Country and city people delight in seeing our pumpkin patch and corn rows fashioned from glowing light bulbs. Our animated barnyard comes complete with sound effects—a crowing rooster and mooing bovine among them.

"Visitors enjoy viewing sentimental favorites in lights—like Santa, his elves and reindeer. Farther on, there are three wise men, a manger scene and an archway of angels."

It's evident that many hands make light work at this powerful country spectacle. Beginning in late October, the couple and their three adult children pitch in with the intricate stringing of bulbs. In addition, some of her craft-minded friends help Kathy deck the barn into a charming holiday gift shop.

"For weeks beforehand, I'm busy canning our harvest-fresh produce," she notes. "When it comes to preserving the

WATTS GOING ON at family farm of Kathy Burt (left) lights up Yuletide lives. Many view beaming scenes from Deere-drawn wagon.

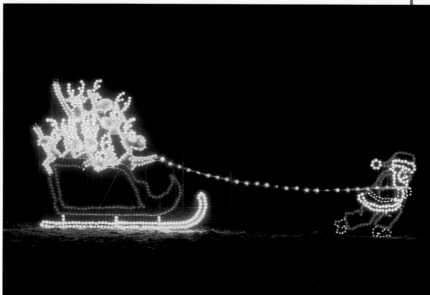

pure goodness of Christmas, we do it in more ways than one."

Indeed, for many of the tens of thousands who trek there annually, this illuminating showcase has become a family tradition. The same can be said for the light-hearted Burt clan.

"Every January, our whole family meets to dream up new, more beautiful displays for the next season," Kathy mentions. "We have three young grandchildren eager to join in the planning, too. So we won't be lacking for energy anytime soon!"

Editor's Note: *The Burts' Appalachian Lights display is open nightly 6-10 p.m. from November 20 through December 30 (closed Christmas Eve). It's located on Highway 52 East about 14 miles north of Dawsonville. Admission is $10 per family vehicle ($12 Friday-Sunday) and $5 per person to tour by hayride. For details, write to Kathy Burt, 4801 Hwy. 52 E, Dawsonville GA 30534. Or phone 1-800/600-2878 (U.S.) or 1-706/265-3701 (Canada).*

TAKING A SHINE to Christmas requires a month's worth of creative juices flowing from Kathy and her clan. Electrifying results range from corny to angelic, prayerful to playful to sacred.

On a Rural Route, Christmastime Came in Brown Paper and Twine

By Doris Brecka of Baraboo, Wisconsin

OVER the last 60-plus years, distances have shrunk while postage prices have shot up. Today, many people routinely carry Christmas gifts with them in the car or on the airplane as they visit family and friends.

Those weren't options back in the mid-1920's, when my married sister lived 150 miles from our family farm. Air travel was out of the question, of course, and auto excursions of that length were reserved for spring or summer.

Instead, we exchanged packages by mail…and enjoyed every minute of it.

On the farm, our preparation began early in autumn with the harvesting of nuts. The pasture contained a dozen or more butternut trees. If we were on our toes, we could easily gather five or six gunnysacks before the squirrels got them.

After being dried, cracked and dried some more, the nuts were stored in glass jars, ready for fruitcake, Christmas cookies and candy. As importantly, several unbreakable containers were filled to put in our parcel to Sister for her own last-minute treats or late-winter baking.

By then, butchering generally was out of the way as well. That meant rings and rings of tantalizing smoked "wurst" made with a mixture of ground beef, pork and seasonings…and "liverwurst", using the liver and head meat, boiled with onion and spices and ground.

After stuffing, both were given several weeks of slow, careful hickory smoking. (I'm sure this part of the package was most avidly received by the man of the family!)

Another welcome gift was a box with sprays of colorful bittersweet (long before they needed to be protected). Sister always said city ladies loved the bright clusters of berries at bazaars. Often, too, a bag of Red Delicious apples was included—if the crop that year had been a good one—along with a bag

of mixed grains for winter feeding of birds and squirrels.

Mama never failed to get our box out in the mail a good week before Christmas, to ensure it would make it to Sister's for the big day. At about the same time, we started the daily watch for *our* package.

By this point in the holiday season, our heavily burdened postal carrier, Mr. Potter, was stopping at our mailbox at 2 or 3 in the afternoon rather than his customary 11 a.m. Mama stationed me in a chair by the front-room glass door with orders to call her on the eagerly anticipated day he got out of his car and headed for the house. That would allow her time to dry her hands and flip off her apron before going to the door to sign for Sister's package to us.

It always seemed like an eternity before that day came. When eventually it did, Mama—exchanging pleasantries with Mr. Potter far too long for my impatient mind—put the package on the dining room table. It never stayed there long!

As soon as my brother was in from school and Dad from early chores, we gathered around to pull away layers of brown paper and strands of twine. Out rolled brightly wrapped packages complete with name tags, stickers and ribbons.

For me, there might be a coloring book, paper dolls or a box of stencils. My brother would have a dollar pocket watch and a jackknife. Mother might get pretty coverall aprons or cherished silk stockings. And Dad might find a box of cigars (something he smoked only on Sunday, relaxing after church and noon dinner).

These days, I realize, some people still *do* send presents. Increasingly, though, they're gifts of money with instructions to "get what you want". That's a sensible solution to modern mailing costs it's hard to argue with.

All the same, no sum could ever buy the excitement watching for "the package" did one lucky little girl long ago!

May you and yours capture the spirit of Christmas... and be captured by it, too.

INDEX 🎀🎀🎀🎀🎀

Food

Crafts

Share Your Holiday Joy!

DO *YOU* celebrate Christmas in a special way? If so, we'd like to know! We're already gathering material for our next *Country Woman Christmas* book. And we need your help!

Do you have a nostalgic holiday-related story to share? Perhaps you have penned a Christmas poem…or a heartwarming fiction story?

Does your family carry on a favorite holiday tradition? Or do you deck your halls in some festive way? Maybe you know of a Christmas-loving country woman others might like to meet?

We're looking for *original* Christmas quilt patterns and craft projects, too, plus homemade Nativities, gingerbread houses, etc. Don't forget to include your best recipes for holiday-favorite main-dish meats, home-baked cookies, candies, breads, etc.!

Send your ideas and photos to "*CW* Christmas Book", 5925 Country Lane, Greendale WI 53129. (Enclose a self-addressed stamped envelope if you'd like materials returned.)